HISTORY OF
POPULAR GARDEN PLANTS
FROM A TO Z

HISTORY OF
POPULAR GARDEN PLANTS
FROM A TO Z

H. G. Witham Fogg

KAYE & WARD · LONDON
A. S. BARNES AND COMPANY
NEW YORK AND SOUTH BRUNSWICK

First published in Great Britain by
Kaye & Ward Ltd
21 New Street, London EC2M 4NT
1976

First published in America by
A.S. Barnes & Co. Inc.
1977

ISBN 0 7182 1140 5 (Great Britain)

ISBN 0 498 02044 4 (USA)
Library of Congress
Catalog Card No. 76 44555

Filmset in VIP Baskerville by Bishopsgate Press Ltd.
Printed in Great Britain by
Whitstable Litho, Whitstable, Kent.

Contents

Section One

1. *Primula veris – the Cowslip*

Going Back in Time

Behind many of the plants, shrubs and trees growing in our gardens today there are stories which, whether sought for or come upon by chance, add much to the pleasure of gardening and often give some indication of cultural requirements.

Some stories reveal human endeavour, even sacrifice; others are rooted in legend and folklore, which is why sometimes they seem to be contradictory.

There are many personalities associated with the early history and hunting of flowering plants. Some of these are recorded in literature centuries old while a few are known only by name. Of others we have more details, but it is from the early seventeenth century onwards that we have the most information, much of which can be found in reference books in the large public libraries. These people include such plant hunters as Banks, Bartram, Forrest, Fortune, Tradescant, Veitch, Wilson and, nearer our time, Kingdon Ward.

Plant hunting is an ancient pursuit, for there is a record of an expedition supported by Queen Hatshepet of Egypt in about 1570 BC, at the time when a new temple was being built. On this journey, to what became known as British Somaliland, both plants and seedlings were discovered and taken back to Egypt. Among the most valuable of these discoveries was the Boswellia tree, from which comes a brittle resin that, when dried, is known as frankincense. The way in which plants are named is no less intriguing. Many of the names were invented centuries ago but are still loved and used today, for instance, Snapdragons for antirrhinums, Granny's Bonnet for aquilegia, Dusty Miller for auricula and Forget-Me-Not for myosotis.

These common names could lead, and have led, to confusion. Frequently more than one name was given to the same subject and sometimes, in different countries the same plant had several common names. This may have been caused by the same subject being named by two different people or a plant thought to be new might have been named at an earlier date. To end this confusion the International Congress took place in Paris in 1854. This established the 'law of priority', which stated that the oldest name given to a plant was the correct one. While this is not foolproof, for changes still occur, it certainly regularises plant naming and, with the foundation of the system of nomenclature laid down by Carl Linnaeus, plant identification is now much easier than it was before.

Although many people still ignore the Latin names of plants and continue to use their common nomenclature or nicknames, we should be grateful that the proper name of a particular subject is nowadays the same in every part of the world, making identification simpler.

As knowledge increases, it is sometimes necessary for botanists to alter the status or position of species within different genera, and detailed literature on this subject becomes available from time to time. It will be found, however, that there is a distinct botanical similarity in the structure of the various species placed within a particular genus even though this may not be immediately obvious.

**John Gerard
1545-1612**

Any consideration of the origin of some of our favourite garden plants must of necessity include mention of John Gerard and John Parkinson, both of whom wrote 'herbals' containing much detailed information not to be found elsewhere.

In the preface to his *The Grete Herball* (1597) Gerard wrote: 'What greater delight is there than to behold the earth apparelled with plants as with a robe of embroidered works set with Orient pearls and garnished with great diversity of rare and costly jewels.' John Gerard, born in Nantwich in 1545, has the distinction of having written what is, even today, the best known of all English herbals from which apt quotations are often made.

Educated at a school near Nantwich, it is supposed that Gerard studied medicine in his youth. We know that, in 1562, he was apprenticed to a Warden of the Barber-Surgeons Company. As a surgeon's apprentice he must have had friends among other apprentices and joined them in their expeditions to collect the herbs which formed the basis of most medical remedies. We know also, from his herbal, that he travelled in Russia, Sweden, Denmark and Poland.

For twenty years he held the post of Superintendent to Lord Burley's gardens in the Strand and at Theobalds in Hertfordshire, and became well known because of his flair for garden design. James I's consort, Anne of Denmark, granted John Gerard a garden in the vicinity of Somerset House for which he paid four pence a year. In his contract it was stated that, in addition to the princely sum of four pence, he was, when required, to supply to his royal landlady 'at the due and proper seasons a convenient proportion and quantitie of herbes, flowers or fruit.' Possibly, in spite of the low rent, the arrangement proved unsatisfactory for he only retained this plot for a year.

Gerard had a house of his own in Holborn and a garden in Fetter Lane, that now rather dismal part of London near Fleet Street. But how wonderful to think that in Gerard's time it was noted for its beautiful houses and gardens. He himself grew more than a thousand different kinds of herbs, though in Gerard's day roses, lilies, gilly flowers and the like were all classed as 'herbs'. He must have collected some of his treasures during his travels abroad for, when writing of his garden and plants, he often mentions that 'these be strangers to England, yet I have them in my garden where they flourish.' He also had many friends and admirers who sent him seeds from Italy, Spain, Syria and the Mediterranean and Jean Robin, in particular, Keeper of the Royal Gardens in Paris, sent him many rare specimens.

Gerard's herbal contains prescriptions to cure most of the ills of the body, as well as a great deal of contemporary folklore. In its pages one finds information about the wild flowers to be found in London in his day, with the old English names of common plants and the reason why such names were given. For instance rest-harrow, so called 'because it maketh the oxen while they be plowing to rest or stand still.'

John Gerard's wife was of great assistance to him in his work, so we are told. He lived, happy in his work and home life, until 1612; and was buried in St Andrew's Church, Holborn.

John Parkinson Born in Nottinghamshire John Parkinson is
1567-1640 regarded as the last of the great English herbalists, but little is known of his life. He was apothecary to James I; and Charles I, on his accession to the throne, gave him the title of Botanicum Regius Prismarius.

Parkinson's best known work is his *Paradisus*, (1629) but he is also the author of *Theatrum*

Botanicum, a stupendous piece of work which took most of his life to write; he did not finish it until he was seventy-three. It is one of the largest herbals written in the English language and describes over 3,800 plants. In it he speaks of his garden in Long Acre, London, and its rare plants.

Part of his letter dedicating *Theatrum Botanicum* to Charles I should be quoted, as it shows the belief then current that illness was due to the enmity of the evil one! He writes:- 'And I doubt not of your Majestyes further care of their bodies health that such workes as deliver approved Remedyes may be divulged, whereby they may both cure and prevent their diseases. Most properly therefore does this Worke belong to your Majesty's patronage both to further and defend that malevolent spirits should not dare to cast forth their venome or aspertions to the prejudice of any, well deserving, but that thereby under God and good direction, all may live in health as well as wealth, peace and Godliness, which God grant and that this boldnesse may be pardoned to your Majestyes loyale subject. Your Servant and Herbalist, John Parkinson.'

John Tradescant 1585-1652 John Tradescant was one of the first of a long line of professional plant collectors. An East Anglian by birth and probably a child of Huguenot refugees from the low countries, much of his life was spent in Kent. He worked for the Earl of Salisbury and then for Lord Wotton. Early in the seventeenth century he became interested in American plants and one which he secured, commonly known as Spiderwort, was officially named by Linnaeus as *Tradescantia virginiana*. He also introduced from the Americas wild flowers – centaureas, lupins and phloxes, which have become favourites in present day gardens.

Subsequently, he travelled to Russia, Algeria and other countries, bringing back various plants and fruit tree stocks, including apricots. He became

gardener to the Duke of Buckingham and later to
Charles I. In 1629 John Tradescant established his
museum surrounded by a physic garden at Lambeth. This was at first known as Tradescant's Ark.
When he died he left the contents of the Museum to
his friend Ashmole, and the collection was passed to
Oxford University, forming the basis of the now well
known Ashmolean Museum.

**John Bartram
1699-1777**

John Bartram's grandfather, a Quaker, had left
Europe in 1682 and settled in Pennsylvania. His
grandson became interested in botany when he was
about ten years old and found great pleasure in
gathering and distributing plants. He bought a plot
of land and experimented in hybridising (this was
subsequently incorporated in the Philadelphia
Botanic Garden). He made several contacts in
England and plants were sent to a number of
influential people, some of whom became his pat-
rons.

Among the plants and trees sent to England, and
particularly to his friend Peter Collinson, were
erythroniums, lilies, gentians, perennial asters and
Liriodendron tulipifera, the tulip tree.

John Bartram's son, William, carried on the work
of plant hunting until he died in 1823.

**Francis Masson
1741-1805**

Francis Masson, a Scotsman, was sent from Kew
Gardens to accompany Captain Cook on his second
voyage in 1772, which took him to the rich flora areas
around Cape Town and the Table Mountains. His
name is commemorated in one of the Cape heathers
Erica massonii. He was able to introduce to Britain
many species of pelargoniums, various heathers, and
nerines; and from the Canary Islands and the West
Indies he collected forms of senecios, some of which
we now know as cinerarias.

**J.R. & J.G.
Forster
1752-1815**

Johann Reinhold Forster and his son Johann Georg,
were two more naturalists who joined Captain Cook
in 1772 on his second voyage of discovery. The older

Forster, who was of German-English descent, had
been trained at Kew Gardens and was a very learned
man although inclined to be a little 'difficult' to deal
with. They found many remarkable plants in South
America and the islands of the South Seas. Among
these were *Phormium tenax*, which produces clumps of
tall iris-like leaves and bronzy-red flowers, *Hebe
elliptica*, *Clematis indivisa* and the well-known palm,
Howea forsteriana, often known as kentia, from the
lonely Lord Howe Island. The success of the
Forsters appears to have led them to extravagance
and they were helped by Sir Joseph Banks, who also
sailed with Captain Cook in 1772, and was probably
the most noted botanist of this period.

**Sir Joseph
Banks
1743-1820**

Sir Joseph Banks, who lived in the reign of George
III, has had a great influence on English gardens.
For more than fifty years he was the honorary
director of the gardens at Kew and responsible for
training men to care for the plants brought back by
collectors whom he had sent to various parts of the
world in search of new species.

Interested in wild flowers from his youth, his
studies were aided by his aquaintance with people
who collected herbs for druggists and by the
possession of an old copy of Gerard's herbal.
Towards the middle of the eighteenth century, he
inherited a large sum of money from his father, and
this enabled him to live near the Physic Garden in
Chelsea and, through his acquaintance with Philip
Miller and other plantsmen of the day, to lay the
foundations of what was to become the Botanical
Gardens at Kew, now of international importance.

In 1772 Sir Joseph sailed with Captain Cook in the
Endeavour to the Pacific and suffered considerable
hardship, which, however, he felt was well worthwhile when he reached his destination. Among the
plants he brought to our notice as the result of that
journey are the *Pernettya* and *Drimys winteri*, although

the latter had first been brought to this country some years earlier.

Banks eventually reached New Zealand, Australia and Java where he found many new forms of plant life. On his return to England he became the Honorary Director of Kew Gardens and, as the result of his efforts at Kew, the first attempts at systematic exploration were planned, with the object of discovering the various flora growing in distant lands.

James Veitch 1752-1839

James Veitch was a Scotsman who moved to Devon toward the end of the eighteenth century and where, after a time, he started a nursery business. The business flourished for well over a hundred years, during which period five members of the family played a prominent part. Almost from the beginning, Veitch sent out plant collectors, including members of his family, to various parts of the world. They made contacts which helped them to discover and bring to Britain a number of treasures, including *Primula obconica, Ranunculus lyallii, Hamamelis mollis* and conifers. John Veitch himself visited Japan in 1860.

Most of these successes took place between 1840 and 1905, the period when James Veitch's son, James, and grandsons, John and Harry, kept the nursery going. (It was at this time too, that William Lobb in California and Chile, and E.H. Wilson in China, made some of their most important discoveries). Unfortunately the business closed in 1914.

David Douglas 1770-1834

David Douglas, the discoverer of the well-known douglas fir, was among the greatest of plant hunters. In 1823 he carried on the work of plant collecting after the death of Sir Joseph Banks and made a number of successful journeys to Hudsons Bay and California. His name is associated with many plants, including *Iris douglasii, Clematis douglasii* and *Limnanthes douglassi*.

His name is also commemorated by a small genus of plants named by Dr. Lindley, although the only species at all well known is *Douglasia laevigata*, an alpine plant which has green foliage and pink flowers. He also found, in British Columbia, the attractive *Mimulus moschatus*. These flowers had strongly scented yellow flowers but, unfortunately, they have now lost their perfume. No explanation can be found for this, since even in their native habitat, the perfume has vanished from the plants.

Robert Fortune 1812-1880
Robert Fortune was born in Berwickshire and worked for a time in the Edinburgh Botanic Gardens before going to London to take up the post of Superintendent of the hothouses of the Horticultural Society's gardens at Chiswick.

In 1843 he went to China, his first base being Hong Kong. Later he moved to Chusan and Shanghai and collected many plants, as well as much interesting information about the people living there. He returned to England in 1846 and for a time was Curator of the Chelsea Physic Garden. Then in 1848 he joined the East India Company and sailed again to China. One object of this journey was to obtain tea plants for introducing to India, a venture not favoured by the Chinese but successful nevertheless.

He made a further two trips. The last one, in 1860, included Japan. He brought back many plants then unknown in Britain and each journey gave him an opportunity to record much useful horticultural information as well as details about the habitat of various plants.

W. & T. Lobb 1814-1885
The brothers William and Thomas Lobb were official plant collectors for the firm of Veitch. Among other subjects, William introduced from Chile *Araucaria araucana*, the monkey puzzle tree; *Berberis darwinii* and *Sinningia speciosa*, better known as the gloxinia.

In 1849 he went to California where his greatest find was the *Wellingtonia*.

Thomas Lobb visited Burma, Malaya and India where he obtained various orchids and a selection of rhododendrons.

Sir J.D. Hooker
1817-1911
One of the greatest botanists of his time, Sir Joseph D. Hooker, although a plant collector, is best known for his output in botanical literature. He was responsible for *Index Kewensis* and collaborated with George Bentham for the *Genera Plantarum*. He was director of Kew Gardens from 1865 to 1885 and became the President of the Royal Society.

George Forrest
1873-1932
The name of George Forrest is held in high esteem among plant collectors. A Scotsman and a keen student, he trained in botany and elementary medicine, studies of great value to him in his later career. He lived in Australia for a few years and also visited South Africa. On returning to Britain he became assistant in the herbarium at Edinburgh Botanic Gardens.

Subsequently, at the request of Mr A.R. Bulley, a founder of the well known firm of Bees Seeds Ltd., he made his first journey to China and also visited Burma and Tibet. Unfortunately Forrest encountered considerable hostility among the natives and he lost the plants that he had collected. However he returned to China in 1910 and again in 1912, and was successful this time in collecting rhododendron seeds and various plant specimens.

E.H. Wilson
1876-1930
It is to E.H. Wilson we owe the discovery, in 1903, of the Chinese *Lilium regale*, now so well known and valued in many countries. He was the keeper of the Arnold Arboretum in Massachusetts and made several successful explorations into China. Although he collected numerous plants and bulbs, he regarded *Lilium regale* among the most important and well worth the personal sufferings he endured to obtain the bulbs.

Dr J.F. Rock
1879-1940

Dr. Joseph F. Rock was a botanist and linguist who at one time held the professorship of the Chinese language at the University of Hawaii. In 1920 he took part in a plant hunting expedition on behalf of the U.S. Department of Agriculture. This took him to Assam, Burma and Siam, his knowledge of oriental languages enabling him to move with ease among the natives.

Subsequently Rock made his home in China from where he made a number of successful plant expeditions. One of his most important discoveries was the Moutan or Tree Paeony. He also found other plants which are now rarely grown, including some excellent omphalodes which are first-class for the alpine house.

Frank
Kingdon-Ward
1885-1958

After taking an honours degree at Christ's College, Cambridge, Frank Kingdon-Ward accepted a teaching post at a school in Shanghai. He was, however, a man who wanted to travel and he became a plant hunter over a very long period; the only interruptions being army service in two world wars.

He was a most particular man and liked to mark plants himself from which seed was to be collected, rather than leaving it to native workers, which was the usual practice. He was an accomplished photographer, keen on mapping and surveying. His journeys took him to Assam, Upper Burma, Tibet and Yunnan.

He married his second wife, Jean Macklin, in 1947 and she accompanied him on several excursions, on one of which a lilium was discovered. This was subsequently named *Lilium mackliniae*. Kingdon-Ward introduced various rhododendrons and berried shrubs and found time to write several excellent books.

Reginald Farrer
1880-1920

A most renowned and successful plant hunter, Reginald Farrer, was born in Yorkshire. In spite of physical disabilities he was a keen gardener and plant collector. He travelled extensively, particularly in upper Burma and China, sending home many valuable plants some of which are now considered indispensable in any good garden. They include alliums, cypripediums, clematis, anemones, gentians, primulas, meconopsis, trollius and dwarf rhododendrons.

His name and fame are commemorated by many plants, particularly alpine subjects including *Gentiana farreri*. He died on a plant expedition in upper Burma where his grave is marked by a plaque erected by his mother, assisted by public authorities.

There are many other names that could be mentioned of persons who have contributed to the introduction of various plants, including Mark Catesby, 1679-1749, who sent various specimens from America; Peter Collinson, 1694-1768, who pestered foreign correspondents to send him seeds and plants and James Lee, 1857-1930, a nurseryman of Hammersmith, who did much to publicise the fuchsia. Augustine Henry, 1857-1930, was a customs and medical officer in the Chinese customs service, who collected plants and sent them to Kew Gardens.

It is because of the interest and labours of these men among many others, that we enjoy the beauty and pleasure of growing many of our most popular garden flowers.

Section Two

2. Anemone

Many of the plants seen in our gardens have an intriguing past, although we seldom pause to consider their origin or how they reached our shores. Some are the result of the work of hybridists who became concerned with improving wild plants found in different parts of the world. Some of these plants were found accidentally; others were discovered through the efforts of missionaries, travellers and plant hunters and soldiers have brought back treasures from foreign wars. Thus many people have worked to enable us to enjoy the beauties of the numerous garden flowers we take so much for granted. Some of these are described in the following pages.

A

Acidanthera This plant of South African origin is closely related to the gladiolus. There are several species of interest and value, but it was not until about thirty years ago that they became really well known in Great Britain. This was the result of the introduction of *Acidanthera bicolor murielae*, a greatly improved form of *Acidanthera bicolor*. The original corms were sent from Abyssinia to James Kelway of Langport, who quickly recognised their value. He records that he was enchanted not only by the grace and beauty of the blooms but also by their strong and attractive fragrance. Captain Erskine sent the corms to England and asked that this new plant should be named after his wife Muriel. This accounts for the fact that it was at first distributed as *Gladiolus murielae*, and it was under this name that it received an R.H.S. Award of Merit in 1932, although it was subsequently identified as an acidanthera.

The corms, which are smaller than those of gladioli and are fibrous coated, do particularly well in pots, the highly scented blooms lasting well when cut for indoor decoration.

Not the least of the attributes of this delightful plant is the fact that it continues to flower over a long period and it is not unusual to cut blooms from the end of July until October. The foliage is typically that of the gladiolus, although a little narrower, while the flower spikes vary in height from 60-75 cm (24-29 in) and bear several large white fragrant flowers, which are blotched purple at the throat. Some attempts have been made to hybridise an acidanthera with a gladiolus and work is still going on with varying results.

Culture is not difficult for, although it was once thought that acidantheras were tender and would only grow under glass, they can in fact be cultivated in exactly the same way as gladioli. They should be planted in April, about 8 cm (3 in) deep, in well-drained soil that contains leaf mould or peat, preferably with the base of the corms resting on silver sand. They are noticeably slow to start in a cold wet soil, so that a favourable site should be selected in the full sun. Acidantheras will not withstand frost: the corms must be taken up in October, when the foliage becomes discoloured. After lifting, the foliage should be allowed to die down, before the corms are laid in trays or boxes in the greenhouse to dry off thoroughly and ripen, preparatory to being stored in a dry frost-proof place for the winter.

As a pot plant *Acidanthera bicolor murielae* is most attractive. Other species sometimes available include *Acidanthera candida* (pure white) and *Acidanthera gunnisi* (white tinged with rose).

Anemone

Also sometimes known as the Wind flower, the name comes from the Greek *anemos*, meaning wind, a reference to its chosen habitat in exposed places, including the slopes of Mount Olympus.

Anemone coronaria, better known as the Poppy Anemone, originated in Asia Minor. In the latter part of the sixteenth century corms of this variety were sent from Constantinople to the renowned Dutch botanist Carolus Clusius (1562-1609), who extensively described the peculiarities of the flowers in many of his writings. He distributed corms among other botanists, as well as among interested friends.

In common with many plants raised from seed, the anemone developed a wide variability and soon innumerable colours were obtained, which contributed to its value.

We know from the English botanist Parkinson, who lived at about the same time as Clusius, that anemones were already cultivated in Holland at the beginning of the seventeenth century. He encouraged his countrymen to sow anemone seeds in the following words: 'Herein lyeth a pretty art, not yet familiarly known to our nation, although it be very frequent in the Lowe Countries, where their industry has bred and nourished up such diversities and varieties. And I doubt not, if we would be as curious as they, but that both our ayre and soyle would produce as great variety as ever hath been seene in the Lowe Countries.' Much later, it proved to be advantageous for English growers to purchase corms from the Netherlands instead, as is apparent from the writings of another famous English botanist John

Justice, who admitted in 1754: 'I must own I never sowed their seeds, because I purchased their roots of the best kind they had in Holland.'

Anemones have always been a prominent feature in various works and descriptions on botany. From such books we learn that the British and French nobility were deeply interested in their cultivation. In the middle of the nineteenth century anemones were sent to France, where a Madame Quetel in Caen (Normandy) cultivated them with great success. From then on anemones gained great popularity in France.

In Holland Poppy Anemones were listed between 1870 and 1880 for the first time under the name of 'Anemone de Caen', which they are still officially called today.

The extent to which anemones were favoured in earlier days may be appreciated from the following anecdote. In about the year 1615, it became known that a certain botanist possessed a marvellous collection of single and double varieties of anemone in as yet unknown colours, which he intended to cultivate for another eight to ten years before parting with them. However, a highly interested person, who had tried in vain many a time to obtain some specimens from this fine collection, went with his valet to visit the botanist and while the two gentlemen were walking in the garden discussing the beautiful anemones, the valet followed behind and trailed the long coat of his master over the flowers thus attaching the fluffy seeds to it.

Anemone coronaria is a colourful and attractive little flower with great commercial value, and it is just as highly prized by the public today as it was in days gone by.

Of the many other species, the following are particularly worthy of note. *Anemone appennina*, which is tuberous rooted, comes from southern Europe and produces sky-blue flowers in March; there are also white and rose varieties. *Anemone blanda* from Greece has deep blue flowers up to 5 cm (2 in) in diameter. *Anemone fulgens* from southern Europe has large solitary flowers of scarlet-crimson. *Anemone nemorosa* is the Wood Anemone, a charming British plant also found in many other European countries. There are forms bearing white, purple and sky blue flowers which appear in April and May. This plant thrives in somewhat shaded positions. *Anemone japonica* is an herbaceous plant which grows 60-75 cm (24-29 in) high and produces its white flowers from September to November. There are a number of named cultivars in white, pink and pale yellow. They flower in ordinary good soil and will grow quite well in semi-shady positions.

Althaea

Many gardeners would not recognise the name *Althaea rosea* as that of the much loved Hollyhock. Several well-known plants belong to this family including the Marsh Mallow (*Althaea officinalis*), and *Althaea frutex*, which is better known as *Hibiscus syriacus*.

The origin of the name hollyhock is a little obscure, but there is reason to believe it comes from the Anglo-Saxon 'holy-hoc' or holy mallow – mallow being a common name given to all members of the althaea family. The word althaea itself comes from the Greek *altheo*, meaning, to cure – a reference to the medicinal virtues of this plant.

The Hollyhock was introduced to Britain in 1573 and, although China is often regarded as its native country, this plant was probably brought to Europe by way of Palestine.

Hollyhocks were grown and valued in Elizabethan days, and in the early half of the nineteenth century various commercial growers took an interest in them. A specialist named Chater of Saffron Walden, Essex, did much to improve the strains then available and Chater's Double has become a strain of high quality, although it is now not quite so readily available because of the ravages of rust disease which attacks all Hollyhocks. This disease first made its appearance in 1873 and soon stopped the plants being as widely grown and exhibited as before. The disease spread from South America to Australia and then to Europe. Some control was obtained by spraying with Burgundy mixture, but for a time Hollyhocks were rarely seen. Now they are returning, both as plants for the cottage garden and for exhibition purposes. Propagation today is largely done by division or seed, rather than by cuttings or grafts as in the past.

Seeds of Chater's Double Mixture are still available. Several new strains have been introduced including Silver Puffs, which grow up to 60 cm (24 in). If sown in warmth in February or March, the plants produce double silvery-pink flowers the same summer. Summer Carnival can be treated similarly, although it is a true perennial strain, growing up to 2 m (6 ft) high. The colour range is wide and this selection was awarded a bronze medal in the All-America Trials.

Antirrhinum The ancestor of the modern antirrhinum is *Antirrhinum majus*, a tall perennial from the Mediterranean region with flowers of varying colours. The shape was once thought to be fashioned like a dragon's mouth, hence the common name of Snapdragon.

This plant was once held in high esteem for its seeds, which yield oil, although they are rarely considered for this purpose today. It is said that antirrhinums came to Britain with the Romans and there is evidence that the plants were naturalised on the cliffs of Dover many centuries ago.

Snapdragons flourish on old walls as the roots apparently like to fix themselves in the mortar. A self-pollinating plant, there are now many species and forms, some with scent and others with more or less double flowers. The seed organs are protected against adverse weather by the unusually shaped corolla, which prevents insects entering until pollination has taken place.

Although the dwarf varieties are excellent for bedding, some of the taller growing hybrids, including Vanguard, have attractive frilly petals and are delicately scented. Several new F1 hybrids are outstanding, including Coronette mixed (60 cm [24 in]), Little Darling (30 cm [12 in]) and Madame Butterfly (60 cm [24 in]), which has the double flowers typical of open-petalled penstemon hybrids. The Rocket hybrids grow to 1.20 m (4 ft) and are the latest development in the tall, base-branching types.

The appearance of antirrhinum rust over forty years ago led to doubt about the plant's future but, as the result of work at Wisley and the experiments of other hybridists, there are now many rust-resistant varieties readily available.

Plants should be raised from seed sown in warmth in the early part of the year. The seedlings should then be hardened off and moved to flowering positions in early May. Later sowings can be made without heat for a late summer and autumn display. They are often treated as annuals, since they look very shabby after coming through the winter. While any good well-drained soil suits these plants, there should be some lime content.

Aquilegia   Commonly known as Columbine, this flower takes its name from the Latin word *columba* (a dove) because the long, narrow, spurred nectaries were thought to resemble the neck of a dove. The name has also been ascribed to *aquila*, the eagle, in reference to the form of the petals. Others prefer to trace the name to *aquilegus* (a water collection) in allusion to the capacity of the flower to hold water.

Poets have frequently referred to the Columbine and it is said that in Tudor times aquilegias were used to help cure sore throats and other ills. Shakespeare makes several references to this plant, as does Homer, too. Certainly, in Elizabethan times it was to be found growing in almost every cottage garden.

Aquilegia vulgaris is reckoned to be a native British plant and is variable in colour, comprising of both single and double flowering forms. *Aquilegia alpina* is a beautiful blue species from the Swiss Alps, while *Aquilegia coerulea* (blue and white) was introduced from the Rocky Mountains well over a hundred years ago. Less common are *Aquilegia glandulosa* (blue and white), *Aquilegia. longissima* (yellow), *Aquilegia skinneri* (yellowish-green) and *Aquilegia viridiflora* (chocolate and green).

Aquilegias do not lend themselves to propagation by division since their rootstock is hard and knotty. It is not necessary to attempt this method of plant increase except in the case of the double varieties, which, generally speaking, are of less elegant appearance. These plants come readily from seed and, since they flower in summer when bees are active, there is little difficulty in getting seed to set. Self-sown seedlings should be weeded out, otherwise the stock soon deteriorates.

Seed is best sown in the open ground in prepared beds as soon as it is ripe but, if you are buying seed, it should be sown in May or early June. Old seed is likely to be slow in germinating. Thin the seedlings early and move them to permanent quarters in the autumn, preferably to somewhere where the soil does not dry out in summer.

Aster   Michaelmas Daisy and Starwort are English names for the group of plants that botanists know as asters, after the Greek word for star. This name does not include the bedding and cut-flower annuals usually referred to as asters, but which are in fact *callistephus*, the China Aster, with which we are not concerned here. A few asters are annuals and a few are biennials but the great majority are perennials.

Asters come from various parts of the world including Europe, Asia, North America, South America and South Africa. They are usually classed in sections, each of which contains varieties having a similar habit of growth. Though all of them are referred to as Michaelmas Daisies, the flowering period is quite extensive and is not confined to Michaelmas. In the past several prominent botanists have objected to asters being given the 'vulgar' title of Michaelmas Daisy, but this name will no doubt continue to be used.

We owe an immense debt to Ernest Ballard, who did so much work on improving the Michaelmas Daisy. He won a First Class Certificate from the R.H.S. for his Beauty of Colwall in 1907. Subsequently he was awarded several similar awards. He raised thousands of seedlings annually but very few came up to his high standards. His patient persistance was rewarded by the many varieties he introduced.

One of the largest groups is that known as *Aster Novi-Belgii*, the aster of New York, where the seed was first collected. Most varieties grow from 1 m (3 ft) to 1.6 m (5 ft) high, although there are a few dwarfs of 15-30 cm (6-12 in). There are single and semi-double varieties in many shades of blue, as well as some red, pink and white named varieties.

Aster amellus is of Italian origin. There are a number of named sorts, notable amongst which is King George; all grow from 45 cm to 80 cm (18-31 in) high and have large daisy-like flowers. They grow best in well-drained soil.

Aster frikartii is a hybrid between *Aster thompsonii*

and *Aster amellus*, while *Aster acris* was brought to
Britain from North America. well over two hundred
years ago. It produces large sprays of lavender-blue
flowers that are useful when cut. Another splendid
species is *Aster ericoides*, which has heath-like flowers
on 30-70 cm (12-28 in) stems and is also useful for
indoor decoration. It grows well in dry soil. *Aster
cordifolius* is similar and bears hundreds of blue
flowers on long sprays well into the autumn.

Aster pappei is often treated as an annual, although
it is a perennial. Growing to a height of 30 cm
(12 in), its blue star-like flowers appear from August
to November.

An inter-generic hybrid known as *Aster luteus*
carries heads of lemon blooms that are excellent for
cutting. Authorities say the correct name is *Solidaster
luteus*.

Aster Novae-Anglae, the New England aster, is
vigorous and healthy, sometimes reaching a height
of more than 3 m (9 ft), especially in rich nourishing
soil. A popular variety in this group is Barr's Pink,
which has full-rayed flowers up to 6 cm (2½ in)
wide. There are other pink, red and blue forms too.

Many other perennial asters are available that
grow from a few centimetres to 2 m (6 ft) high. Some
types like moist conditions and all of them like sun.
Propagation is easy, usually from simple division,
but cuttings are successful and in many cases seed
can be used, although the resulting plants will vary
in colour and habit.

B

Begonia

The history of this plant starts with Plumier, the
early botanist and monk. He is credited with the
discovery in 1690 of the begonia in Mexico. The
plant he found could not be placed in any known
genus and Plumier, as he had done with other

discoveries, in naming them after someone whom he admired, decided to bring into being a new genus. This was named after Michel Begon, a French botanist, who was also governor of Santa Domingo. Thus the name 'begonia' came into being.

It was not, however, until the eighteenth century was well advanced that the begonia was first seen in Britain, when a plant arrived at Kew Gardens. Subsequently, others came from both the West and East Indies. There was no real interest or advance in knowledge of the begonia, though, until the second decade of the nineteenth century. At the end of a further forty years, many species were known, including some which we still hold dear such as *Begonia evansiana*, *Begonia maculata* and *Begonia gracilis*.

Britain has not been the only country interested in the genus: work on hybridising has been carried out in several countries, including the United States of America. It was the apparently accidental discovery of *Begonia rex*, with its colourful metallic-looking leaves, in a box of other plants just over one hundred years ago which raised the genus to a higher status in the eyes of horticulturists. From this time on it was not only men of substance and those able to travel who were interested in the begonia but the average gardener as well.

It is not only Mexico and the Indies which have played a part in the history of this lovely plant, for it is true to say that Peru, Bolivia and other parts of South America also have many wild species, while there are some in Africa and the Himalayas too. It appears that the first substantial shipment of the tuberous varieties took place in 1847. They were sent from Bolivia to the London firm of Henderson. It was, however, another shipment from the same country, part of which came into the hands of James Veitch, a member of that once renowned firm of plant growers and distributors, which made begonias popular. Veitch exhibited the plants at flower shows both in London and Paris, where they attracted great attention. It is believed that the begonia in question was *Begonia boliviensis*, which has bright red flowers.

Various crosses were made between this species and others, resulting in some good hybrids. One which can still be found in specialised collections is *Begonia sedeni*, which is named after John Seden, who was employed by Messrs Veitch and who made a number of successful crosses. *Begonia sedeni* is the result of crossing *Begonia boliviensis* with an undisclosed Andean species. The result of this first cross was not only important in itself but also because it is the basis on which the modern hybrids have been built.

Other early species which were much used in hybridising and in which some of the characteristics of the tuberous begonia of today may be seen include *Begonia pearcei* and *Begonia veitchii*, brought into prominence by Richard Pearce, who travelled for the firm of James Veitch of Chelsea. The fact that *Begonia veitchii*, in its native habitat grows in partially shaded fairly moist woodland glades and at high altitudes together with the fact that both *Begonia pearcei* and *Begonia veitchii* were largely used in hybridising, is some guide as to why tuberous begonias can be grown so successfully under widely differing conditions. We may assume that most of the yellow and near yellow present-day tuberous hybrids have their origin in *Begonia pearcei*, while the stocky growth and large flowers of our best sorts have come through *Begonia veitchii*.

Another Veitch development was *Begonia rosaeflora*, which has also been much used for hybridising. *Begonia davisii* was introduced from Peru and has given much to the basic qualities of good modern forms.

All this time breeders in other countries were working on the begonia with a measure of success and fresh species were being found in South America. One, *Begonia baumanni*, was introduced by Lemoine, the famous French breeder. This came from Bolivia and was sent by Lemoine to a German plant specialist named Baumann, after whom it was named. A feature of *Begonia baumanni* was its large size and its sweet scent. It is unfortunate that the fragrance has not proved to be a dominant quality, although there have been just a few hybrids that have emitted some perfume – these, I believe, are from crosses based on *Begonia baumanni*.

At first, all the begonias available produced single flowers; subsequently, plants were raised that had flowers with many more petals. Although the first ones were of little use due to poor constitution or because they were in some other way undesirable, Lemoine was eventually able to distribute a double tuberous begonia. This was a good hybrid of which *Bogonia boliviensis* was one of the parents.

There are various cane-stemmed species and varieties which are propagated from cuttings. Of the fibrous-rooted begonias, the winter flowering Gloire de Lorraine and its varieties are the best known. They were raised by the French plant breeder Victor Lemoine nearly one hundred years ago. Gloire de Lorraine is the result of a cross between *Begonia socotrana* and *Begonia dregei*.

From the species *Begonia semperflorens* have come a large number of named hybrids very suitable for summer bedding, some of which have beautiful glossy bronze foliage, giving rise to the title of Wax Begonia. These can be raised easily from seed sown in warmth early in the year.

Bellis perennis There are dozens of plants which have the word Daisy as part of their common names. The real or original Daisy is *Bellis perennis*, which is rarely held in the esteem it deserves. It has been referred to as Day's Eye, since the flowers close with the approach of evening.

Its Latin title, *bellis*, means pretty, although there are other derivations, some arising from the fact that the juice of the roots was at one time used for healing wounds, particularly those of soldiers wounded in battle, and for bringing out bruises. This is why bellis plants once had the common name of Bruisewort. Daisies have also figured in woodwork, in tapestry and in the arms of royal personages.

They flower for a long time, which is why they have been used so much in gardens. The older semi-double varieties are less popular than the full-double flowering cultivars, which are ideal for window boxes and tubs.

Dresden China with its quite small shell-pink buttons has long been popular, although newer varieties are taking its place, including Double Pomponette Mixed in shades of red, pink and white, the flowers of which are 3 cm (1 in) in diameter and have pretty quilled petals. Bright Carpet is a compact strain producing fully double flowers in several shades on 15 cm (6 in) stems. Of the same size, Haubner's Fairy Carpet, Rose and Red, produce neat plants of uniform habit. A species known as *Bellis prolifera* is better known as Hen and Chickens from its habit of sometimes sending out miniature flowers from the central blossoms; another common name is Jack-an-apes on Horseback.

Propagation is by division of plants in June, or by seed sown in boxes in April or in the open ground in May and June. The seedlings should be in their flowering positions by October.

C

Calendula

This name comes from the Latin word *calendae*, meaning first day of the month. Calendulas are sometimes looked upon as a plant for the cottage garden and are even scorned by some people as weeds, yet a flower that has survived six centuries surely deserves a small place in any garden. They are still widely known as Marigolds, which is really the common name for the so-called French and African tagetes.

3. Calendula – the Pot Marigold

Shakespeare immortalised calendulas in his well-known lines 'And winking mary-buds begin to ope their golden eyes', but the 'mary-buds' were winking many years before. In this country they have been traced as far back as the thirteenth century. Today calendula is often known as the Pot Marigold, a name not half as charming as Mary-Bud or their other name, Mary-Gold, arising from legend.

A charming story says that many years ago there lived a beautiful golden-haired child called Mary Gold. She spent all her time sitting watching the sun, until one day she disappeared and was never found again. In the place where she used to sit there sprung a little sun-like flower. Friends proclaimed it was really Mary Gold and that she had been changed into a flower like the sun she loved so much.

In Devon and Wiltshire Marigolds were known as Drunkards. It was said in these parts long ago that, should you pick a Marigold or even look at it for a short time, you would turn to drink! The people of Wales, however, treated it more kindly; to them it was a weather prophet, for it was believed that if the petals did not open before seven o'clock in the morning, there would be rain or even a thunderstorm.

Apart from legend and superstition, Marigolds held an important place in the early medical world. They were used against fever, children's ailments, ulcers, varicose veins and to give relief from bee or wasp stings. Women also acclaimed them for beauty purposes; their petals were supposed to impart a yellow colour to hair. In domestic circles their petals were used to flavour soups and stews: 'Fair is the mary gold for pottage meat', says John Gay in the *Shepherd's Week*. We can still find in books today instructions for drying Marigolds for seasoning.

Calendulas are easily raised from seed sown in the open ground where the plants are to flower. Although the main sowing time is in the spring, if seed is sown in September, the flowers will appear much earlier. It is essential to remove self-sown seedlings from around plants which have been established for some years, otherwise the stock deteriorates.

Capparis spinosa This is a slightly tender evergreen shrub, from which the flower buds are pickled and used as capers; they have a mildly pungent flavour and are used in sauces and pickles. Nasturtium seeds are sometimes used as a substitute for capers and, while they are useful for this purpose, they do not approach capparis in quality.

First introduced into Britain in the late sixteenth century, capparis has long been cultivated from Greece through Yugoslavia and Italy to Southern France and Spain, in which areas the plant sometimes succeeds out of doors in warm sheltered places.

Once established, these plants will for many years bear a large crop of young flower buds from May to September. These are harvested daily before they become large and lose their flavour. They are then allowed to wilt for a few hours in the sun, before being immersed in salty-vinegar, which is changed weekly for a few months.

Seed is available in this country and can be sown from February to September in pots of sandy compost, or cuttings can be taken from established plants. As they develop, the plants become rather a tangle of intertwining branches, which are armed with spiny stipules.

Capparis sandwichiana, with much larger, creamy flowers and orange pods is a native of the Hawaiian Islands, but seed of this species is rarely available.

Cheiranthus cheiri
Better known as the Wallflower, this is one of the most ancient plants and its exact origin cannot be traced. The generic name comes from the Greek *cheir* (the hand) and *anthos* (a flower) in allusion to the general use of the flowers as nosegays.

A native of Southern Europe, it is impossible to determine how or when Wallflowers were first cultivated. It may very well be that they were brought to Britain during the time of the Romans. Certainly as early as the late fifthteenth century it was fairly well-known and had a number of common names including the Bee Flower, Wall Gilleflower and Bloody Warrior, the latter confirming that it may have been brought by men of war from distant places in Europe. It is said that a sprig of Wallflowers was once worn by young men in their caps as a sign of their constancy to their girlfriends at home.

This flower has always been the symbol of fidelity.

The outstanding characteristic of the old Wallflower was that, like most of the modern varieties, it was very fragrant and much has been written about it. Francis Bacon wrote of the, 'sweet scent which delights the heart and perfumes the air and (Wallflowers) are delightful to be set under a parlour or tower chamber window.'

Wallflowers can sometimes be found growing on limestone cliffs or on ancient walls. These plants are usually a bright yellow, although there are many brownish-red forms, and undoubtedly red and yellow were the colours of the original strains. Today scented Wallflowers are available in many shades including pink, ruby, orange-red, carmine-rose, white, cream, ruby-violet and scarlet, whilst there are also many delightful pastel shades in separate colours and mixtures.

Hybridists in Britain, the United States and other countries have produced greatly improved strains, and there are now varieties producing double flowers as well as a very dwarf selection flowering from late March onwards.

The orange Siberian Wallflower, *Cheiranthus allionii* and its yellow, lemon and apricot forms are also excellent, growing to about 30 cm (12 in) high. In addition *Cheiranthus linifolius* forms compact bushes with mauve flowers. The seed of all varieties can be sown outdoors in May and June, and the plants may be put into their flowering quarters in the autumn.

Chrysanthemum Few flowers are now more highly valued or widely grown than chrysanthemums. It is commonly believed that this plant was first cultivated in Japan, but it was in fact in China that the plant originated. Ancient records show that it was mentioned by Confucius about five hundred years before Christ. While there are indications of the refinement and beauty of these ancient chrysanthemum species, they cannot be compared with modern varieties. Little was done by the Chinese to improve the flower, although they did endeavour to retain it.

The modern cultivated chrysanthemum is now recognised under the name of *Chrysanthemum morifolium*, although its exact ancestors cannot be identified. In view of the centuries that have passed since the first mention of the plant was made, this is hardly surprising. We do know, however, that *Chrysanthemum sinense* and *Chrysanthemum indicum* have played an important part in the development of the flower. One wonders why the name *indicum* was given, since the species in question is a native of China and Japan, and apparently is not a wild species in India as the name suggests. Both species are of bushy habit and have single white and yellow flowers respectively. The foliage of both closely resembles that of the modern cultivated forms.

It was about the year AD 386 that the chrysanthemum first reached Japan, apparently via Korea. Even then, it was not widely distributed and it was more than 250 years before the Japanese took an active interest in the plants. By selection and cross-fertilisation with some of the wild Japanese species, the flower gained importance.

Towards the end of the eighth century, the chrysanthemum became the national emblem of Japan and the highest honour that could be bestowed upon a citizen was the Order of the Chrysanthemum. The design of the flower became the official mark on all state documents and was used as a sign or crest for imperial purposes. The Japanese chrysanthemum of centuries ago bore little resemblance to our modern sorts: the fragile, wiry stems easily responded to training.

Chrysanthemum shows or festivals began in Japan in about AD 900 and continued for fifty years.

They were started by the Emperor Uda, which gave the flower the highest possible standing. Until recently, one of the best and largest types of chrysanthemums was known as the Japanese Section; now they are referred to as Large Exhibition varieties.

The earliest record of chrysanthemums in Europe was made in 1688 by Bregnius, a Dutchman, who was a botanist and a writer, though it was not until a century later that the chrysanthemum became established in England. It came via France, where it had been taken by a Frenchman called Captain Louis Pierre Blanchard. Of his varieties brought from China, only one survived.

In about 1795, plants of the first variety to succeed in Europe were sent to Kew Gardens and became known as Old Purple. At this time, too, the scientific name of *Chrysanthemum morifolium*, now applied to the late flowering varieties, was given to the plant. Other varieties came to England from China and by 1826 more than fifty different varieties were in cultivation. The first European chrysanthemum show was held in Austria in 1831. Enthusiasts then formed groups to promote the cultivation of this plant in Britain. The Norwich and Norfolk Chrysanthemum Society was formed, and soon after 1829 groups or societies were started in Birmingham and Swansea. In 1846 what was to become the National Chrysanthemum Society was formed at Stoke Newington.

Earlier, there had been several men prominently concerned with the flower: John Salter raised improved varieties, and in 1843 the famous Robert Fortune was sent to China by the Royal Horticultural Society. Among other species he sent home the Chusan Daisy, from which has come the modern Pompone varieties. Later Fortune visited Japan and sent to Britain a collection of choice varieties. Robert Fortune's second journey brought to light the first

Japanese varieties which had reflexed petals. Other pioneers who brought the chrysanthemum into prominence include Simon Delaux of Toulouse and Dr Walcott of the U.S.A.

The chrysanthemum is yet another example of a simple flower being taken in hand by hybridists and transformed into something altogether superior. As a cut flower, pot plant, greenhouse subject or for growing in a window box the chrysanthemum is altogether dependable. Many less common types have been raised during the past fifty years including the Lilliputs, Cascades and Charms, while we must not forget the Koreans and the many annual varieties.

Convallaria This is the Latin name of Lily of the Valley, suggesting that the plant grows in valleys. This is a good indication of its preference for moisture and partial shade, although of course it will not succeed in water-logged conditions. The old Lily of the Valley, *Convallaria majalis*, is reckoned to be a native of Britain, although it is now rare in the wild state. There are also a number of other species and forms which, however, are much less well-known.

Having long been of interest to growers in Germany, the first mention of Lily of the Valley in the botanical agendas of that country was in 1826. The original centre of commercial cultivation of the crowns was around the old town of Wittenburg, where, from the year 1860, exports of considerable size were made to England and Holland, and it is evident that the wide forest lands surrounding the town were a good natural source of supply.

Although the pure white Lily of the Valley is the only well-known variety nowadays, there is reason to believe that early in the nineteenth century, there were pink and red sorts in the forest, as well as an unusual double red form which appears practically unknown today and for which there is no source known to the author.

In addition to *Convallaria majalis* with its several forms, *Convallaria globosa* and its two varieties, *japonica* and *latifolia*, can sometimes be obtained, as well as *Convallaria alba marginata striata*, which has attractive variegated foliage.

The Lily of the Valley is an attractive plant for the garden, the cold frame, and for pots in the living room or greenhouse. In Somerset it was once known as Lady's Tears, a name that came from the legend that these highly scented flowers with white bells sprang up originally where the Virgin Mary's tears fell to the ground.

Another Sussex legend has it that Lily of the Valley grew where the blood of St Leonard was shed during his battle with a dragon in a forest near the town of St Leonard's, where the flower once grew profusely. It is certainly true that the bells hang as if in mourning, although the green leaves help to make them attractive.

These plants were once thought to be a sign of death if they were accidentally seen in bloom, while centuries ago in some country places it was supposed to be harmful, if not dangerous, to plant Lily of the Valley, for the planter was likely to die within the next year.

On the other hand, *Convallaria majalis* was believed to have various beneficial medicinal values such as improving a poor memory, relieving gout and clearing eye inflamations. The dried flowers are still used as an ingredient in eye medicine, though there is sound reason for believing that extract of Lily of the Valley is very poisonous and it must, therefore, only be used by those with knowledge of its dangers.

Culture is extremely simple: the pips or crowns can be planted out-doors in early November in a semi-shaded position rich in humus matter. Forcing crowns are often available for growing in pots in the greenhouse, while retarded crowns, which have actually been frozen, can be potted and will produce their flowers within three or four weeks of planting – this makes them valuable for Christmas and New Year display and scent.

Crocus In some of the ancient languages of the East where the vowels were not given as much attention as the consonants the word was written K.R.K.M. and there are various renderings of this such as karkum and kurkum. Eventually this word was used by the Greeks as *krocos* and was subsequently latinised as *crocus* by the Romans.

It is the autumn flowering *Crocus sativus* which has a most intriguing history. The famous Gerard speaks of the crocus as the true saffron and says, 'the floure of the saffron doth first rise out of the ground nakedly in September and his long small grassie leaves shortly after, never bearing floure and leaf at once. The floure consisteth of six small blew leaves tending to purple having in the middle small yellow strings or threds; among which are two, three or more thicke fat chives of a fierie colour somewhat reddish, of a strong smell when they are dried which doth stuffe and trouble the head.'

Nothing is really known of the home or origin of *Crocus sativus*. It is said by some that it was brought to Britain by the Romans, but an old and more interesting story suggests that it was introduced into England by Sir Thomas Smith of Saffron Walden in about 1330. A writer in the sixteenth century records that a traveller on his journey to Turkey said, 'Saffron, the best of the universal world groweth in this realm. It is a spice that has cordial and may be used in meats and is excellent in dyeing of yellow silks. This commodity being Saffron groweth in Tripoli on a high hyll. It is said that from that hyll there passeth yearly of that commodity 15 moiles laden with that commodity.' It is said in Saffron

Walden that a pilgrim, intending to do good to his country, stole a head of crocus saffron and hid it in his staff, which he had made hollow for the purpose. Thus he was able to bring the root to England, although it was at the risk of his life for he knew that, if he had been discovered, he would have been executed. It is, however, from this venture that the foundation of the saffron industry was laid at Saffron Walden centuries ago. It is a remarkable thing that no fewer than 4,300 of the threadlike stigmas were needed to produce an ounce of the dry raw material.

In an old herbal we are told that: 'Saffron will destroy all manners of abominations of man's stomack and will make a man sleep. It is good for medicines and for cooks to colour their meat. It grows in gardens and is hot and dry.' During the reign of Henry VIII a law was passed prohibiting the dying of linen with saffron since the dyed sheets were not washed often enough. There are many other old beliefs about saffron and one writer advised his readers to mix it with dragon's blood, camomile flowers, swallows' nests, worm-eaten wood and the fat of a mountain mouse!

Saffron was also at one time used as an ingredient in cakes, etc. Again to quote from an old book: 'If men had drunk saffron they need never fear from the overwhelming of the brain. Saffron keepeth them from drunkenness and maketh them carry their drink well.'

Crocus speciosus is now one of the most widely-grown autumn-flowering species. Its blue-mauve or lavender blue flowers have a reddish-orange stigma and yellow anthers. *Crocus kotschyanus* is similar. From these species have come a number of good forms including *Crocus aitchisonii* and *Crocus cassiope*, which are both bluish-lavender, and *Crocus oxonion*, which is a fairly deep blue.

There are many winter and early spring flowering

crocuses which make it possible to pick flowers on Christmas Day, when the weather is not freezing. *Crocus chrysanthus* from Greece and Asia Minor is a species which has given rise to a wide range of seedlings – many of these were raised by the famous E.H. Bowles. *Crocus imperati*, named after a famous Italian botanist of the sixteenth century, has yellowish-buff flowers that are shaded and veined in lilac-mauve. The spring flowering crocuses show colour from February till the end of March – one of the best is *Crocus sieberi*, which has several forms, most with lilac-mauve flowers marked yellow or orange.

The so-called garden crocuses were raised in Holland. They are most adaptable for all parts of the garden, grassland and, providing they are not forced, for pots and bowls. Cultivation is simple: a sheltered sunny situation, where the ground is in good condition, should be chosen. At least 5 cm (2 in) of soil should cover the corms.

D

Dahlia variabilis

This is a variable species of dahlia, which accounts for its name, and it is commonly believed to have been the first one to have been introduced to this country. A native of Mexico and Central America, it received its generic name from Dr Dahl, a Swedish botanist and pupil of Linnaeus. The earliest known description of the dahlia is that of Francesco Hernandez, physician to Phillip II of Spain, who wrote in 1615 the first of four books entitled *The Plants and Animals of New Spain*; and in one of these books appears an illustration of *Dahlia variabilis*. Then, for a space of 130 years, the dahlia seems to have been lost to writers until 1787, when a Frenchman, one Nicholas Joseph Thierry de

Menonville, was sent to America to secure the
cóchineal insect and in that year published a treatise
in which he described the dahlias he had seen in a
garden near Guaxaca.

'In the year 1789 Vincentes Cervantes, director of
the Botanic Garden at Mexico, forwarded seeds of
the dahlia to the Royal Gardens at Madrid, then
under the direction of Abbé Cavanilles. The Mar-
quis of Bute was at this time Ambassador from
England to the Court of Spain, and the Marchioness,
who cherished a true sympathy with floriculture,
obtained some of these seeds, which she cultivated in
pots in a greenhouse, but failed to keep them beyond
two or three years'.

'In 1802 an English nurseryman, John Fraser of
Sloane Square, a collector of American plants,
obtained from Paris some seeds of *Dahlia coccinea*,
which flowered in a greenhouse in 1803 at his
nursery, and supplied a subject for a plate in the
Botanical Magazine, which secured to the plant a
proper place in the English Garden.'

It is believed that in 1804 Lady Holland, who was
then in Madrid, sent home seeds to Holland House,
Kensington, where plants were raised and came into
bloom. Though these plants were lost, a third stock
was brought from France in 1815. It is thought that
these flowers showed signs of doubling, for from this
date double dahlias began to appear.

From then on many types of dahlias were
developed including the show and fancy forms,
Pompone or Bouquet types, and in 1880 the Cactus
dahlia appeared. This was named *Dahlia juarezi* after
a President of Mexico. There are now additional
sections such as Tom Thumb, Quilled or Anemone
flowered, Collerette and Orchid flowered.

Apart from the impressive large flowering varieties which are so valuable for garden decoration
and for exhibition, there are many strains which are

invaluable for summer bedding. While many of these can be propagated from cuttings in the usual way, strong plants will be ready for their flowering quarters from early June onwards if seed is sown in warmth in February and will continue to bloom until frosts come. Such types include Coltness Hybrids, Ideal Bedding and the newer strains such as Early Bird and Redskin, the latter being a spectacular development as they have bronze foliage and semi-double flowers in a range of lovely colours. Once frost has cut down the foliage, the tubers should be lifted and, after being thoroughly dried, they should be stored in a frost-proof place until the following early spring.

All dahlias can be propagated by division of tubers or from cuttings, and seed is becoming another recognised form of increasing stock, although only in a very few cases can any degree of trueness be assured.

Delphinium   The ancient Greeks gave this name to the flower for they saw in the unopened buds some resemblance to the dolphin, the likeness of which is still preserved in many of the most modern varieties. At various times the delphinium has been known as the King's Spur, and the Little Spur, while Larkspur is still used for the well-known annual delphinium. The use of the name Larkspur to describe the family seems to have originated in England, for the sixteenth-century writer John Gerard says in his herbal 'that in England the plant is known as larks spur, larks heel, larks toes, larks clawe and munkeshoode'. It is easy to see that the horn-shaped nectary of the flower resembles the spur of a lark's claw. John Parkinson made several references to the delphinium in his *Paradisus Terrestis* of 1840.

There are many species, which come from such widely distant places as the Himalayas, Siberia, China, Afghanistan, Ethiopia and California. It is only during the last 120 years or so that the work of hybridising *Delphinium elatum* has been carried out in Britain and other countries, both by professional and amateur growers. One of the most notable occurrences was in 1921 when Watkin Samuel staged a remarkable exhibit of the flowers at the Chelsea Flower Show. The broad based pyramidal spikes were a great improvement on all the then known varieties.

Nearly forty years ago the West of the Rockies red strain was raised and introduced by A.A. Samuelson of Pullman, Washington, U.S.A. This came from a collection of species which were mostly natives of the western United States.

The Bishop and Pacific Giant strains are now well-known as, of course, are the marvellous sorts raised and exhibited by Messrs Blackmore & Langdon. We now have varieties producing flowers in almost every shade of blue, mauve and purple, plus attractive combinations of these shades. In the Pacific Giant strains in particular there are shades of colour not to be found elsewhere, including lilac, pink, raspberry, rose, pure white and white with black or brown centres.

The Belladonna section of delphiniums consists of the small flowered types, which produce spikes from 30-45 cm (12-18 in) high. The named varieties of these vary in colour in many shades of blue, as well as white and pink.   Species which are undoubtedly having a great effect on producing new varieties include *Delphinium nudicaule* and *Delphinium cardinale*, which are both red, and *Delphinium zalil*, which is yellow.

Delphiniums will grow on most soils which contain lime. In well-cultivated ground that is rich in humus early spring is the best planting time, although in well-drained unexposed situations the plants move satisfactorily from early October to the middle of November. The roots should be well spread out and fine soil worked around them. For the tall varieties some kind of support will be necessary and for exhibition flowers a few applications of dried blood will be helpful. Named varieties may be propagated from cuttings when shoots of 8-10 cm (3-4 in) can be secured or selected plants can be carefully divided.

Dianthus   This is the correct name of the large family of plants which we know best under the names of Carnations and Pinks of which there are perennial and annual varieties. The word dianthus comes from the Greek *dios* (devine) and *anthos* (flower). *Dianthus caryophyllis* is the Carnation and the epithet means 'cut leaved', a reference to the shape of the foliage.

Carnation flowers were once used to flavour wine, hence another of their names, Sops in Wine. Some very old writings suggest that Gillyflower was another common name of the Carnation, but this title is more aptly applied to the Wallflower. Many varieties have picotee edgings and this word comes from the French *picoté* – marked or pricked with colour markings at the edge of the petals.

The term 'clove' Carnation was originally applied because some of the earlier varieties had the smell of the Indian Clove tree, *Caryophyllus aromaticus*. This may account for Chaucer's reference to 'Giliflowers and nutmeg to put in ale'.

The popularity of Carnations is apparent from John Gerard, who wrote, 'Every climate and country bringeth forth new sorts'. The National Carnation and Picotee Society was formed during the middle of the nineteenth century.

Dianthus plumarius is one of the parents of the so-called 'Pink', which was introduced from Normandy in about the year 1100. Its flowers are smaller than those of the carnation, and its petals are more toothed and are borne on shorter stems. *Dianthus caesius*, often known as the Cheddar Pink, is the species which grows naturally on limestone soils. *Dianthus deltoides*, the Maiden Pink, is also widely used in rock gardens.

It is not always easy to discover how the various sections of the Carnation family have evolved from the original types, but newer varieties have certainly been created as the result of hybridising during the last hundred years.

Border Carnations are the oldest type. They were and are classed according to their colour markings. These include Selfs, Picotees, Bizarres, Flakes, Cloves, yellow and white grounds. They flower outdoors during summer, although some exhibitors grow the plants in a cold greenhouse or frame. Cottage Carnations are hardy, having come from the old English and Scottish border varieties; of dwarf habit, they freely produce flowers. Perpetual Flowering Carnations are sometimes known as Tree Carnations or American Carnations. They grow best in a moderately heated greenhouse, although they can be cultivated in a cold greenhouse, too.

Border Pinks and Laced Pinks are old garden plants and flower from early summer onwards. They flourish in ordinary good garden soil.

Many dianthus hybrids have been raised during the last fifty years, and a number of first-class strains and groups have been created by the firm of Allwood Brothers at their Sussex nurseries. One such variety is *Dianthus allwoodii*, the result of crossing the Perpetual Flowering Carnation and the hardy Border Pink. This robust plant flowers from spring to winter; if covered with a cloche, it will produce blooms in December. *Dianthus allwoodii alpinus* is a hybrid suitable for rock gardens.

Dianthus Sweet Wivelsfield flowers outdoors from June to October. This is the result of crossing *Dianthus allwoodii* and *Dianthus barbatus*, the Sweet William, and can be raised from seed sown in heat early in the year to flower in the same summer and autumn. Alternatively, it can be treated as a biennial by sowing in August and September, so that it flowers the following year.

Dianthus Delight is a fairly new hybrid, which has come from a cross between an alpine species and Dianthus Sweet Wivelsfield. Dianthus Rainbow x Loveliness is a hybrid between Sweet Wivelsfield and *Dianthus speciosa*, while Dianthus x Sweetness is the result of a cross between Sweet Wivelsfield and Loveliness.

The so-called Mule Pinks are a hybrid from garden dianthus crossed with Border Carnations and Sweet Williams. The most widely-grown Pinks today are Mrs Sinkins (white), named after the wife of the master of Slough Workhouse, Inchmery (pale pink) and Painted Lady (pink and white). Of much more recent introduction is the double-flowered Yellow Hammer, raised by Montague Allwood by crossing *Dianthus knappii* with *Dianthus allwoodii* seedlings.

There are a number of annual carnations which provide a grand display. These are usually offered in seedsmen's catalogues as Marguerite and Chabaud Carnations.

Carnations are easily propagated from pipings or cuttings inserted in sandy compost in a temperature of 15°-18°C. Most pinks can be increased by division or cuttings, while the annual Carnations as well as the Chabauds and Enfant de Nice can be raised from seed sown in warmth in January or February. After germination, the seedlings should be grown under cool conditions – 12°-15°C will be quite sufficient.

Dianthus barbatus   This old-fashioned flower has the common name of Sweet William, which is said to have various origins. One suggestion is that it was a tribute to William the Conqueror, for the plants were said to grow 'aplenty in the hills of Normandy'. Another suggestion is that

it may have been named in honour of William of
Aquitaine (St William), while others have thought
the name was a tribute to William Shakespeare, who
seemed to have a high opinion of the flowers 'for
decking gardens as well as personal adornment'.

Although there is little scent in some strains,
typically Sweet Williams have a rich clove perfume,
which, with their bright colours, makes them most
showy. The Latin epithet (*barbatus*) is given because
of the hairy scales of the calyx.

Sweet Williams, although they are perennials, are
usually treated as biennials. Seed can be sown in
boxes under glass in the early spring and then the
seedlings can be hardened off and planted outdoors
in May or, even simpler, seed can be sown in open
ground beds in May or June. The young plants
should be in position by October for flowering the
following year.

Strains now available in separate colours include
Pink Beauty, Scarlet Beauty and Crimson Velvet,
while there are several superb mixtures including
the Auricula-Eyed and Double strains. A dwarf
mixture, growing only 15 cm (6 in) high, is excellent
for border edgings. Recently some annual strains
have become available, notably Wee Willie, a
mixture growing 10-15 cm (4-6 in), and a mixture
up to 30 cm (12 in) high.

**Dicentra
spectabilis**

This name comes from two Latin words: *dis* (twice)
and *kentron* (spur), an allusion to the double-spurred
flowers. First brought to Britain from China in 1810
and then lost, this plant was re-introduced from
North America by the plant hunter, Robert Fortune
in 1846. It soon achieved popularity both as a garden
plant and as a greenhouse subject. Throughout the
years, it has accumulated a number of vernacular
names, all of which arise from the shape of the
flowers. Among these are Bleeding Heart, Lyre
Flower, Lady's Locket, Dutchman's Breeches and

Our Lady in a Bath.

This plant has received the highest honour the Royal Horticultural Society can bestow – the Award of Merit. The glaucous-grey deeply-cut foliage and arching sprays of crimson and white locket-shaped flowers are most attractive. If a flower is plucked, turned upside down and the two 'wings' gently pulled apart, it immediately becomes apparent why one of its common names is Lady in the Bath (or Boat).

Plants of this species can be forced into early flowering by keeping them in a moist atmosphere in a temperature around 12°C.

There are several other good species available, including *Dicentra cucullaria*, which is no more than 15 cm (6 in) high, *Dicentra eximia*, 20-40 cm (8-16 in) and *Dicentra formosa*, which grows to 15 cm (6 in) with prettily divided leaves.

Although dicentras may suffer if grown in heavy ground and during unusually wet cold winters, once they are established in deep well-drained soil, they will give great pleasure for many years. The roots must not dry out in summer.

Plants can be increased readily by dividing the crowns in early spring or by cutting the fleshy roots into short lengths and inserting them in sandy soil in spring.

Digitalis It is not easy to discover why this old English flower has the common name of Foxglove. It seems likely that Foxglove has no connection at all with the nocturnal marauder who, if given the opportunity, works havoc among sleepy fowls. It is probable that Foxglove is a corruption of 'folks glove' and that the folk are not human beings but the 'little folk' or fairies, who, if such mysteries are to be believed, might very well get into Foxglove flowers and hide there. Other people say that, since the flowers can be likened in shape to a finger-stall or a 'glove' to protect an injured finger, the connection is obvious, especially as the botanical title (digitalis) comes from a Latin word meaning finger protector. This lends authority to the suggestion that the common name should be Fairy's Glove.

Foxgloves can be found growing wild in various parts of Great Britain and they are excellent plants for semi-shady positions where choicer subjects will not grow. While they flourish in low lying positions, they do not object to higher sites so long as they have moisture.

Digitalis ambigua (or *grandiflora*) is the most common species and has yellowish flowers. *Digitalis davisiana* has unusual bronze flowers and *Digitalis mertonensis*, which grows to 75 cm (30 in), has exceptionally large flowers in a crushed strawberry shade. As the result of careful selection, several fairly new types have been evolved, notably the Excelsior Strain, which grows to a height of 1.60 m (5 ft). Its flowers, carried horizontally around the stem, are spotted in shades of cream, primrose, pink and purple. Foxy, 1.25 m (4 ft), has flowers of many colours spotted with maroon; this selection can be sown in heat early in the year.

Foxgloves are usually grown as biennials, although they seed very freely, so there are always a number of new plants developing. Little skill is needed to raise the plants from seed sown in prepared beds of fine soil in May or early June. The seedlings should be thinned out before they become crowded and transplanted to flowering quarters in October.

E

Euphorbia   This is the botanical name of a very large genus of plants best known as the Spurges. There are believed to be more than one thousand species distributed in various parts of the world. They vary greatly in appearance ranging from weeds to quite large shrubs.

One of the best-known and widely-used as a greenhouse and living room plant is *Euphorbia pulcherrima*. This was first seen at an exhibition in Pennsylvania in 1829, when it was shown as *Poinsettia pulcherrima*, having been named in honour of Dr J.R. Poinsett, who discovered it in Mexico. As a wild plant there, it was not at first recognised as a euphorbia.

Because its scarlet bracts provide colour at Christmas (the flowers being insignificant), breeders have taken this plant in hand and the Mikkelson strain was created. Intensive breeding has led to Mikkelpink, while there are several others in varying shades of red. Further efforts on the part of plant hunters and breeders have resulted in many other euphorbias becoming available, amongst which is *Euphorbia splendens* from Madagascar, known as the Crown of Thorns because of its long branched spurs. It needs a winter temperature of 8°-10°C.

There are quite a number of species which can be grown in the garden, one good annual or biennial being *Euphorbia heterophylla*, which has branching stems of 50-60 cm that culminate in a whorl of showy red bracts. *Euphorbia marginata* is known as Snow on the Mountain and its pale green leaves and white bracts make it useful for floral decorations as well as for buttonholes.

Euphorbia wulfenii is also well-known: it received an R.H.S. Award of Merit in 1905. Its stems of glaucous green leaves are surmounted by terminal heads of greenish-yellow flowers. *Euphorbia pilosa* is of neat habit with bright golden bracts in spring and its leaves turn a handsome bronze in autumn. *Euphorbia amygdaloides variegata* has showy foliage and so, too, has the form known as *chaxiana*. *Euphorbia cyparissias* is known as the Cypress Spurge and is a native of Europe, including Britain. It grows 30 cm (12 in) high and during April and May produces slender grass-like leaves and quite small greenish-yellow flowers, which are surmounted by bright yellow bracts. *Euphorbia epithymoides* or *polychrome* is the Cushion Spurge and produces its round flower heads topped by sulphur-yellow bracts during April. Although it only grows to about 30-38 cm (12-15 in) high, it has possibilities for cutting. *Euphorbia sikkimensis* is a good plant for the border and deserves to be better known; it produces yellow flowers from July to September on 1 m (3 ft) stems.

Most of the euphorbias have milky stems which contain sap and should, therefore, be cut with care so that the strength of the plant is not lost. The annual varieties are easily raised from seed and grow in any ordinary good soil.

F

Freesia

The derivation of this name is unknown although it may commemorate a botanist by the name of Frees. One of the earliest references to the freesia is in a book on plants by an Austrian botanist published in 1790, when it was referred to as *Gladiolus refractus*. Later it was listed as a tritonia, while another authority placed it in the genera ixia. It was not until about 1866 that a decision was made that it should be a separate genera and be named to commemorate Frederick Freese, a German doctor who was keen on horticultural matters.

Freesia refracta was for a long time the only species available. Its soft creamy-yellow flowers were sweetly scented. Subsequently other species came into cultivation and were used for crossing with

Freesia refracta, resulting in many coloured hybrids. These, however, were not particularly outstanding.

Gradually breeders in Italy, France and Holland became interested in this subject, and several fine strains were introduced. A number of British hybridists were highly successful and two of them, G.H. Dalrymple and F.M. Chapman, introduced hybrids which have made a great contribution to varieties now in cultivation. More recently, the Parego Horticultural Company of Spalding and Messrs Jan de Graaf of Holland have done valuable work in making freesias easier to grow.

Today, there are many named varieties in cultivation, which must be grown from corms since they do not come true from seed. Seeds of hybrids sown in warmth in spring will produce flowering plants from September onwards but, for winter blooming, corms should be planted in pots of sandy soil from mid-July onwards. They must not be forced.

It is now possible to grow freesias outdoors by planting prepared corms from mid-April onwards, selecting a warm, well drained position.

Fritillaria Comparatively little has been written about fritillarias but the genus has been in cultivation for centuries. Records as far back as 1570 show pictures of various forms, including *Fritillaria imperialis*, *Fritillaria meleagris* and *Fritillaria persica*. John Gerard made mention of them in his famous herbal as did Clusius early in the sixteenth century, while John Tradescant bought bulbs in Holland to take to Britain. Gerard, in particular, praised them 'for the beautifying of our gardens and the bosums of the beautiful'.

Fritillarias comprise a large genus with a wide distribution from the Mediterranean to China and through to North America. While the majority are easy to cultivate, the few that are difficult are worth growing for their subtle beauty.

The name fritillary appears to have originated from the supposed likeness between the flower and a square on a chess board, which apparently was once known as a fritillus. Another attractive common name is Ginny-hen or Guinea-hen Flower on account of the checkered markings on some of the species. This plant was, in fact, once known as the Checkered Daffodil.

Of the many species now available the following can be relied upon. *Fritillaria cirrhosa*, which in spring produces stems 45-60 cm (18-24 in) high with flowers of purplish-brown with greenish or yellowish shadings. *Fritillaria imperialis*, better known as the Crown Imperial, is reckoned to be one of our oldest cultivated plants and grows in European gardens as well as in the high altitudes of India, Persia and Afghanistan. In spring it produces several yellow flowers on stems 1-1.50 m (3-4½ ft) high, terminating in a tuft of leaves. There are orange and red forms. The scaly bulbs, up to 15 cm (6 in) thick, emit a strong unpleasant foxy smell when handled. An old legend says that this flower refused to bow its head when our Lord passed on his way to Calvary and the pendant bells, with unshed tears found in the nectaries, are a lasting token of regret and repentance.

Fritillaria meleagris is the Snakes-head fritillary, a native of European countries. In spring two or three flowers are carried on 22-25 cm (9-10 in) stems in varying shades of rosy-purple with checkered markings. This gives rise to the other common name of Guinea-hen flower. This species and its varieties such as Artemis (smoky-purple) and Charon (deep purple) are excellent for growing in pots. *Fritillaria pyrenaica* is a hardy species and easy to grow. In April, it produces purplish-brown flowers checkered with crimson-purple and yellow on stems that are 20-30 cm (8-12 in) high. *Fritillaria pudica*, for the alpine house, has large nodding yellow bells on 15 cm (6 in) stems in April.

Fritillarias like moist soil that contains plenty of leaf mould, but the soil must not remain wet in winter or the bulbs may rot. Some of the less common species grow on stony ground, where drainage is sharp.

Fuchsia

The natural habitat of the fuchsia is Mexico, Central and South America, and the Andes, while a few species are from New Zealand and one or two other places. Even so, this plant is considerably hardier than might be expected and no doubt some of this hardiness is due to the considerable amount of hybridising which has been carried out over the years.

Like the geranium, the iris and other favourite plants, the fuchsia has a very interesting past. The first extant reference to the plant, as far as can be traced, is in a book by Père Plumier published in 1703 that contains a description and a drawing made after a journey to America. The plant is referred to as *Fuchsia triphylla flore coccinea*. Plumier named the plant he found in honour of Leonhart Fuchs, who lived between 1501 and 1566. Fuchs occupied the chair of Medicine at Tübingen University in Germany and was also a botanist of repute. He was the author of several books, including one important volume (*Historia Stirpium*) dealing with about five hundred different species of plants which were known in Germany and other countries. The fuchsia was not included, but Plumier admired Fuchs and his works, and so named the plant he found in honour of him.

The arrival of the fuchsia in Britain is rather shrouded in mystery. There seems sufficient evidence to believe that *Fuchsia magellanica* from Chile and *Fuchsia coccinea* from Brazil were at Kew as early as 1788. This, however, rather spoils the romantic story which has for long been believed about how the fuchsia came to Britain. According to the story James Lee, a nurseryman, saw the first fuchsia in a cottage window at Wapping in the East End of London. He asked to purchase the plant, but the owner, a woman, refused to sell the plant, saying that it had been brought home by her sailor husband (son) on his last journey from South America. Lee, however, determined to get the plant, offered a price so high that it proved tempting to the woman, who sold it to him. The story says that the buyer was able to obtain three hundred cuttings from the plant after only one year, and furthermore, was able to sell each one for a guinea a time. It seems probable, however, that the story of the sailor was put out as a cover for the 'transferring', somehow or other, of the plant from Kew Gardens to Lee's nursery, since it was only four or five years after the first record of their being at Kew that Lee had plants for sale!

We do know for certain that from the end of the eighteenth century onwards many additional species were introduced to this country. A large number of hybrids and varieties appeared, many no doubt raised from seed. At a conservative estimate about one hundred fuchsia species have to date been found, but the number of hybrids raised is well over two thousand. This does not mean though that all the latter are available today.

The fuchsia may truly be called an old-fashioned plant, but it is certainly not out of date. Together with some other subjects that in the past were once widely grown, it did for a time go out of favour. It is once again firmly established as a most desirable plant for greenhouse, living room, garden, verandah, window-box or hanging basket, while it is not now unusual for it to be included in special bouquets. These uses will give some idea of the versatility of the fuchsia.

A plant of easy cultivation, it is rarely attacked by pests and is hardly ever affected by disease. Generally free flowering, it has a tremendously wide colour range and yet is never gaudy; its quiet dignity always compels attention.

As time advances and newer sorts appear, some of the older varieties disappear, although there are some available today which have been in cultivation for sixty years and more. It is interesting to recall the tremendous advance which has been made in regard to colour, for, whereas the majority of the older sorts were shades of red, nowadays the colour range takes in blue, mauve, lavender, purple, orange, cream, white, pink and a tremendous number of reds, including scarlet, carmine, crimson and coral. In some, there are traces of green, too, as well as many delicate pastel shades. Reference to the catalogues of specialist growers will reveal the many attractive varieties now available, not only those which can be grown in the greenhouse or living room but also the so-called hardy varieties such as *Fuchsia gracilis*, which has scarlet sepals and purple corolla, and *Fuchsia magellanica* and its varieties, including Madame Cornelissen (semi-double scarlet and white) and the hardiest of all, *Fuchsia riccartonii*. These hardy varieties are usually cut down to ground level in winter but make rapid new growth in the spring.

Galanthus nivalis

Snowdrops are less commonly known as Candlemas Bells, because they normally come into flower around the first few days of February, the time of Candlemas, which in the Church calendar is the feast of the purification of the Virgin Mary. This was also once considered to be the end of the Christmas festivities, when the decorations and greenery were taken down. Other names once used for the Snowdrop were Purification Flower, Mary's Tapers and Milk Flower.

This plant was once regarded as being unlucky and one record refers to it as Deaths' Flower, for it was believed by some people that, if a single flower was brought indoors, a death would follow. This is somewhat odd, since at another period, taking Snowdrops indoors was said to act as a protection against evil.

Galanthus nivalis, the common British Snowdrop, has several forms including the double *Galanthus nivalis flore pleno*, *Galanthus nivalis scharlokii* and *Galanthus nivalis viridapicis*. *Galanthus imperati* flowers early in January. *Galanthus elwesii* has broad reflexing leaves and flowers tipped with green. *Galanthus plicatus* forms large bulbs and flowers in March.

As a result of interest in this lovely flower, a number of newer hybrids have been raised. These include *Galanthus Fosteri*, *Galanthus Colesbourne* and *Galanthus G.S. Arnott*, the latter growing 25-30 cm (10-12 in) high.

Less common than all these is *Galanthus olgae*, a Grecian Snowdrop, which flowers in September and October. *Galanthus octobrensis* from Albania blooms in October and November, and *Galanthus rachelae* often blooms in November and early December.

Contrary to usual practice, Snowdrops can be moved in May when the foliage is green. The majority of suppliers, however, still offer them while they are dormant and the bulbs should be planted 8-10 cm deep. Once planted in good well-drained soil in a border, rock garden, shrubbery or grassy area, Snowdrops can be left to look after themselves.

Gentiana   This plant is a native of several countries including China, Burma, India and Tibet. There have been a number of plant-hunting expeditions to these countries, all of which have yielded their treasures. Some species have been known and named for centuries.

Oddly enough, it was not the beauty of these plants that gave them their original popularity, but their supposed or real curative powers which ensured them a place in medicinal prescriptions. King Gentius of Illyria in the Adriatic, who gave his name to this family of plants, is said to have benefited from the use of the bitter roots, while another legend says that Ladislaus, King of Hungary in the mid fifteenth century, asked God to show him a herb that would help this stricken people and he was guided to a gentian.

Later it was believed that ground powdered roots, particularly those of *Gentiana lutea*, counteracted the effect of bites from dogs and other beasts. It was also recommended as a refreshing drink when the powdered root had been steeped in water and, because of its bitterness, as an 'antidote to love'.

Two of the best known species are *Gentiana acaulis*, which in the spring produces deep blue bell-shaped flowers, and *Gentiana sino-ornata*, which does not like lime and produces funnel-shaped royal-blue flowers in the autumn. Their erratic flowering sometimes discourages gardeners, for occasionally they bloom profusely and at other times fail to show colour despite every attention. They can be grown in pots and tubs as well as in the rock garden.

Gentians are hardy and should be given a place out of the shade, away from the drip from trees, and where the soil remains moist without being wet.

Gladiolus

The gladiolus derives its name from the Latin *gladius* (sword) in deference to the shape of its leaves. The genus contains more than 150 species and hybrids, all with sword-like ribbed leaves and spikes of flowers, having three larger upper perianth segments and three lower ones, nearly always spotted or marked. It is not possible to indicate all the species and hybrids, but those referred to below are among the most important and have had the greatest influence on the development of the gladiolus as we know it today.

Gladiolus gandavensis was probably the earliest type to be introduced for garden use and was developed by hybridising the wild species. It was known in Belgium as early as 1837, where it probably originated. After its introduction to Britain it soon became popular. The blooms, which appear rather late, are scarlet with a lighter stripe down the centre of each petal.

Ten years later, the variety known as *Gladiolus brenchleyensis* was raised in Britain. This was rather more vermilion in colour than *Gladiolus gandavensis*, and its flowers were not quite so close to each other along the spike. Not only were there developments in Belgium and England but in France too. The renowned nursery of Lemoine at Nancy, famed for lilacs, produced *Gladiolus lemoinei*. Its blooms of various colours are made conspicuous by throat markings or blotches in strikingly contrasting shades. A few years after this break-through, the Lemoine nursery produced *Gladiolus nancianus*, which was larger than *Gladiolus lemoinei* and its flowers opened wider.

Gladiolus saundersii was another species that came into being around the middle of the nineteenth century. It grows 75-90 cm (30-36 in) high and in early autumn produces spikes of large crimson-scarlet flowers, marked and stippled with pink and white.

Germany, too, produced a new gladiolus: the well-known *Gladiolus childsii* (the result of crossing *Gladiolus saundersii* and *Gladiolus gandavensis*) was raised by Max Leichtlin, who gave his name to several other subjects including camassias. The stock was purchased by Mr Childs of the United States, who renamed it and introduced it as *Gladiolus childsii*. This hybrid grows 60 cm (24 in) high and has bright red flowers the lower segments of which are yellow marked with red. Undoubtedly this is among the forerunners of the present large-flowered gladioli, although *Gladiolus childsii* itself varies considerably in habit and colour.

Gladiolus ramosus flowers from July to September and, although it is seldom mentioned, is an excellent sort. It bears flowers in many shades of rose-pink and red marked and feathered with white, and often produces branched spikes.

Not so hardy as the species so far mentioned, *Gladiolus cardinalis* is particularly fine; in July and August it produces large scarlet blooms, each of which has a white blotch on its lower segment.

Gladiolus tristis from South Africa grows only about 45 cm (18 in) high. Its large flowers on graceful stems, produced during June and July, are creamy-primrose. The upper petals are spotted or marked with brownish-green and the blooms are beautifully fragrant. *Gradiolus psittacinus*, another South African species, has large rich scarlet flowers with yellow lines and spots; both stems and leaves grow strongly and it is probable that this species is one of the parents of *Gladiolus gandavensis* hybrids.

Turkey has given us *Gladiolus byzantinus*, which produces brilliant wine-red flowers on 60 cm (24 in) spikes in June and July. It will grow in any well-drained garden soil and looks good when naturalised. It is hardy and can be planted in October or November.

Gladiolus cuspidatus has whitish flowers, the lower segments of which are marked with purplish-red, while *Gladiolus quartinianus* of African origin grows about 90 cm (36 in) high and produces yellow flowers marked and spotted with scarlet.

Much better known is *Gladiolus colvillii*, a hybrid between *Gladiolus cardinalis* and *Gladiolus tristis*. Growing about 60 cm (24 in) high, its dainty crimson-purple flowers are flaked with white. There are numerous forms of *Gladiolus colvillii* which are hardy in all areas that are not cold or exposed; they flower from the end of May.

Gladiolus primulinus is one of the most recently introduced species. It has, in fact, had a tremendous influence on the development of the present day varieties. This species was found growing in the rain forest near the Victoria Falls on the Zambesi River in 1902. It was sent to England by Francis Fox whose firm of architects built the bridge at the falls. The flowers of this wild species were smaller than any of the other groups, their blooms being set further apart on thick wiry stems. This resulted in a very much lighter and daintier appearance, and the yellow flowers are very noticeable, which is undoubtedly why the flower first caught the eye of Mr Fox.

A peculiarity of the petal formation of *Gladiolus primulinus* is that its top petal curls over rather like a hood. This is reckoned by botanists to be Nature's way of guarding the pistils and stamens from the misty spray which is continuous in the original habitat of this plant. It has been aptly named Maid of the Mist. After many generations there are now scores, if not hundreds, of named primulinus hybrids, all of which have come from the original corms. Although the hood is still present, it is much less pronounced. This species has introduced many new shades into the large-flowered varieties and other strains that are not available commercially.

The most widely grown gladioli today are the large-flowered primulinus Butterfly and Miniature varieties. All of these varieties flourish in good soil containing plenty of humus matter and which retains moisture.

Gloxinia   This plant is named in honour of P.B. Gloxin of Strasburg, Germany, and the first records of it appeared in 1785, although it was not until 1817 that the plant was introduced to England, when it was named *Gloxinia speciosa*. In 1825, however, botanists discovered that the gloxinia had been wrongly named. Technically speaking, it was not a gloxinia but a gesneriad belonging to the genus *sinningia*. Its original name had become popular so that few people today know the plant by its supposedly correct title.

The gloxinia or sinningia originated in Brazil and the earliest one known in cultivation was *Gloxinia maculate*. Then followed *Gloxinia speciosa*. This plant had small nodding purple-blue flowers. The flower tube or corolla protruded to make the so-called Slipper Blossom. Subsequently a breeding programme was started and many varieties were introduced, some self-coloured and others beautifully speckled. A number of named hybrids are now in cultivation and they make excellent pot plants in the greenhouse or living room.

The colours range from pure white to the deepest crimson, and bright fiery red through to purple, violet, rose and pink. In addition to the self colours, there are many exquisite forms beautifully speckled and edged with colours distinct from the ground-work. Now that gloxinias can be raised easily from seed, more charming colour combinations are being produced. Flowering plants can be secured within six or seven months of sowing in warmth. The tubers can be started into growth from January in a temperature of 15°-20°C, using a peaty loam. Leave the top just exposed so that moisture does not settle in the depression on the top side of the tuber.

H

Hyacinthus

Hyacinthus, in Greek mythology, was the son of the Spartan King Amyclas. He was a youth of great beauty and was loved both by Apollo and by Zephyr. One day, when Apollo was teaching Hyacinthus how to throw the discus, Zephyr in her jealousy threw the discus against the head of Hyacinthus and killed him. Apollo, unable to bring him back to life, made a flower grow from Hyacinthus's blood in memory of him. This flower, however, was not the Hyacinth we know today and the story is almost forgotten. But the fragrant, well-loved and colourful bloom we call the Hyacinth is gaining in popularity year by year, all over the world.

4. Hyacynthus

The Hyacinth was brought to western Europe from Asia Minor centuries ago, in about 1560. In the year 1612 Besler described thirteen colour variations of the single Hyacinth and three of the double. The double type did not become very popular, but we can truly say that the single Hyacinth has become the 'Queen of the bulb family'. Since 1700 it has been used as a garden plant. Originally only blue and white Hyacinths were known, but after 1740 red and pink were introduced, and after 1760 even yellow varieties came into being.

Like the Tulip, the Hyacinth was at one time the object of frenzied trading, as it was considered to be a fashionable flower to have in the garden. Even Madame de Pompadour favoured the Hyacinth and Louis XV ordered between 6,000 and 8,000 livres' worth of bulbs every year from the Dutch bulb growers. An order dated 1759 has been found which mentions 363 Hyacinth bulbs for flower beds and 200 for Hyacinth glasses.

After the Napoleonic era the trade changed; prices were more reasonable, the forcing varieties were popular and came to the fore, and the trade became more wholesale. In England the Hyacinth became very popular and in 1861 the Horticultural Society of Edinburgh announced a Grand Hyacinth and Spring Flower Show. In Liverpool, Newcastle-on-Tyne and elsewhere, Hyacinth shows were held. In other countries, too, Hyacinths gained fashionable acclaim: in Austraia and Germany the plants were bought in large numbers, and large quantities of top size bulbs were exported to Russia for winter forcing.

Hyacinths are still extremely popular for growing in pots and bowls. By careful selection of varieties, colour can be provided over a period of many weeks, especially nowadays. Commencing with Romans and following these with the Herald and prepared types, which are succeeded in turn by untreated bulbs, you can have constant blooms indoors from mid-November until April. Hyacinth bulbs planted outdoors in September and October will produce a colourful display from mid-March onwards.

I

Iris   The word 'iris' can be simply interpreted as the 'eye'. The iris family consists of about 200 species and a very large number of varieties. The genus includes herbaceous plants with fleshy or woody root-stocks, others with rhizomes and a large group which are bulbous. There are irises which grow only a few centimetres high, while others grow up to 1.80 m (6 ft). Fortunately the family has been conveniently divided into groups with certain characteristics.

Much of the popularity of this family is due to the careful patient work of hybridists over many years. The remarkable thing is that, although the home of many irises is in countries as far apart as Spain, China, Austria, the United States, Persia and South Africa, if properly provided with simple requirements, most irises will grow and flourish in Britain and other countries that have a similar climate.

Although the iris has become better known and more valued during the last century, it has a very long history, for some varieties have been used and written about for many centuries. The first written reference to it was in the fourth century BC by Hippocrates. The flower in some form or other has often been portrayed in paintings, pottery, embroidery and heraldic designs. It has been held in much esteem by religious orders and *Iris pseudacorous* is thought by some experts to be the subject originally referred to as the Fleur-de-Lys, which was the heraldic flower on the arms of the French Kings. Among the many legends of how the plant acquired its name the most widely accepted is that concerning Clovis, King of the Franks. At some time during the sixth century, by the river Rhine near Cologne, Clovis was hemmed in by a number of Goths. He noticed some yellow irises growing in the centre of the river bed and realised that the water was shallow at that point. Thus he was able to cross the river and escape from his enemies. Henceforth the iris was adopted as the badge of the French Royal Family.

Many years later, Louis XII of France adopted the same plant as his emblem and it became the Fleur de Louis. The name was gradually corrupted to Fleur de Lys.

The dried roots of many types of iris were frequently used for medical purposes and extracts from the rhizomes were used in the making of drugs, oils and perfumes, as well as for healing wounds and sores. In addition, the rhizomes of *Iris florentine* and others have long been used for making orris root. The selected rhizomes are lifted after the plants have flowered, cut into thin layers and laid out to dry. Drying brings out the perfume, which is rather like that of Violets. The thoroughly dried slices are put into little sachets, which may be placed in a linen cupboard, where the pleasing fragrance permeates the contents.

It is not always clear which are the actual varieties depicted in old illustrations and handiwork, for even today, in spite of the large amount of information available, there are still problems over the nomenclature and synonomy of the iris.

Although the iris of earlier times was very different from the modern sorts, and the colour tones we now have could hardly have been dreamt of centuries ago, we can be certain that this flower, which has had a glorious past, is still capable of further development.

From the information available it is certain that the tall bearded irises have come from crosses between species which are not generally available today; these include *Iris cypriana* and *Iris mesopotamia*, neither of which are hardy in our climatic conditions. Some of the earlier hybrids of these species did not respond too well to culture in this country, but among the qualities which were passed on to subsequent hybrids were the large flowers and long stems of the two species mentioned. The result has been that, by the use of these hybrids in breeding, size has increased and the colour range considerably extended.

W.R. Dykes (1859-1925) will always be remem-

bered in the iris world. He was a man whose
knowledge of the genus was profound: his great
monograph on the family *The Genus Iris* is indeed a
classic, while his small volumes are full of factual
information. *Iris W.R. Dykes* was the first large-
flowered yellow and it has had a great influence on
all the modern yellow sorts.

Fifty years ago another *Iris germanica* or Flag Iris
came into being which has altogether altered the
purple and violet-blue shades and has led to an
improvement of the petal texture of other colours
too: this was the variety Dominion raised by A.J.
Bliss, an amateur iris grower. The pale velvety falls
of this variety have introduced a quality into the
petals which made them more attractive than the
earlier sorts.

Iris Gudrun, raised by Mrs Dykes, has been widely
used in the production of better white sorts. Raisers
in America and France have done much work on
irises, and the former in particular have had success
with their creations. Other outstanding people who
in the past have done much for the iris include: G.P.
Baker, George Yeld, Amos Perry, Sir Cedric Morris,
Mrs Murrell, Mrs Anley and Sir Michael Foster who
were all British and Grace Sturtevant and William
Mohr who were American. Sir Michael Foster did
much patient work in improving the tall bearded iris
though he also had tremendous knowledge regarding the bulbous types.

Being natives of Persia and Syria, the oncocyclus
group of irises require just a little more attention
than the other groups. They like well-drained sandy
soil and a warm sunny situation. The irregularly
shaped rhizomes should be planted up to 8 cm (3 in)
deep in October. The flowers of all oncocyclus irises
are very striking. Among the best are: *Iris susiana*,
which is named after the Persian word for iris and is
silvery grey with purple spots flushed lilac on a

creamy ground; *Iris gatesii*, which has immense flowers of pearly grey; and *Iris lorteti*, which has falls of creamy-yellow with crimson spots and white standards veined in violet.

Iris kaempferi is the Japanese iris so valuable for growing near the edge of a stream, pond or lake.

Almost all the bulbous irises are of easy culture. *Iris reticulata* (violet-blue) and its many hybrids (23 cm [9 in]) gain their name from the reticulated network of fibres on the bulbs. They flower early and like well-drained soil, as does *Iris danfordiae* (yellow).

The so-called English irises, *Iris xiphioides*, come from the Pyrenees. These, together with the Spanish and Dutch irises are excellent for cutting as they grow from 45-60 cm (18-24 in) high.

All irises should be planted in September or October. Their beautiful colouring from May onwards make them outstanding in any garden.

Isatis tinctoria This is the ancient botanical Greek name of the plant from which woad was made. In Caesar's commentaries on the Gallic Wars he said that 'all the Britons, without exception, stain themselves with woad (vitrum) which gives them a blue colour and makes their appearance more terrible in battle.' Pliny the Elder referred to 'a plant like plantain, with which the wives and daughters of the Britons paint their bodies in certain ceremonies, which they attend coloured like Ethiopians.'

The source from which the ancient Britons obtained their woad is not known with certainty. The plant was not native to Britain, although some writers give the impression that it had been cultivated here from very early times. It was probably native to south-eastern Europe from whence it spread to other parts of the world. Samples of mummy cloths dyed with indigo have been found in Egypt and it is possible that the dye came from woad. By the middle Ages woad-dyeing had become a flourishing industry. The plant was cultivated extensively in France, Germany and Italy, and dried paste made from it was imported into Britain in large quantities.

Ancient documents refer to the woad trade between Amiens and Corby, and Amiens and Norwich in 1286 and London in 1334. A customs document refers to dues levied on woad imports and the same roll mentions the importation of casks of 'wayd' from Amiens in 1302. From then until the end of the sixteenth century the woad industry flourished. The plant was cultivated extensively on the Continent, principally in Germany, France and Italy, and much wealth was derived from it.

The chief woad-growing centres in England were in Lincolnshire and Cambridgeshire. There was also a centre at Glastonbury. The saying 'as blue as woad' survived in East Anglia until about a century ago. Records differ about the colour produced. In some cases it was said to be blue, in others green, and again in others black, hence the reference to Ethiopians. This is not so contradictory as it appears, since all these colours can be produced from the woad plant, depending on the method used. True indigo blue is the dye common to the Woad plant (*Isatis tinctoria*) and the Indigo plant (*Indigofera tinctoria*). It forms as a scum on the surface of the vessel or vat in which the dye is being made. It may be that our ancestors obtained the dye in this way. The juice of fresh woad leaves will produce a lasting black dye when rubbed on the skin, and the stain only disappears with the growth of new skin.

This plant produces blue-green leaves from a compact root-stock and sends up stems 1 m (3 ft) high, bearing clear yellow flowers. It thrives in almost any good soil including fairly dry positions. Best grown as a biennial, propagation is from seed sown in spring.

J

Jasminum   Whether it is grown as a bushy plant or as a climber, this is a most attractive subject. Jasminums are attractive because of their delicate fragrance and their elegant, slender semi-trumpet-shaped flowers. The derivation of the name itself is not difficult to trace, for behind the English name jasmine, we have the Arabic *ysmyn* and the Persian *yasmin*. In old literature it is sometimes referred to as Jessamine.

Jasminum officinale, the sweet white Jasmine, is a native of the East Indies and is deliciously scented. This is the species which was often referred to by poets such as Cowper and Moore.

Jasminum nudiflorum is the semi-shrubby yellow winter-flowering Jasmine introduced from China in 1844. It prefers a little shelter, but even in exposed places it bursts into bloom during mild spells. It is valuable for north walls.

Several other species are available including: *Jasminum revolutum* with dainty compound foliage and yellow flowers; *Jasminum beesianum*, a scandent climber with rather small crimson flowers; *Jasminum humile*, a semi-evergreen. 90-1.20 m (3-4 ft) high carrying bright yellow flowers in late summer; and *Jasminum stephanense*, which grows strongly and has fragrant pink blooms throughout the summer followed by black berries.

All Jasmines like rich loamy soil. They can be propagated from 10 cm (4 in) cuttings of semi-ripe wood inserted in sandy soil in late summer in a close frame or in open ground in autumn. After flowering, cut out old badly-placed wood. The winter-flowering Jasmine in particular should be well pruned back since it blooms most profusely on new wood.

K

Kniphofia

Named after J.H. Kniphof, an eighteenth century German professor of medicine, this genus of handsome plants comes mostly from South and East Africa. They have the common names of Red Hot Poker and Torch Lily as the smooth, heavy stems are surmounted by many elongated brightly-coloured flowers which, when seen among dark foliage or in the twilight, stand out as flaming torches. They are hardy plants, although at one time they were regarded as somewhat tender, probably because they came from Africa.

They remain evergreen during winter, but the leaves are inclined to flop or spread out. This makes it easy for rain to get into the crowns. If it then freezes, the plants may suffer permanent damage, since the tender tissues inside the crown would be destroyed. This is why in winter it is advisable to pull the leaves together, fastening them so that rain and cold do not penetrate the centre of the plants.

Kniphofia caulescens is particularly good, producing 1.30 m (4½ ft) spikes of salmon-red. *Kniphofia galpinii* has vivid flame-coloured torches from July to September. It is best grown in a well-drained sheltered position. *Kniphofia nelsoni* has narrow leaves and bright scarlet flowers on 60 cm (24 in) stems from August onwards.

Kniphofia macowanii only grows to a height of 45 cm (18 in) and has tight brush-like spikes from July to September. *Kniphofia uvaria* is the species from which a large number of splendid hybrids have been bred including Goldese, which has tapering spikes of soft yellow; Kathleen, which is greenish-yellow; Royal Standard, which is red and yellow; and Star of Baden, which is a rich yellow. Work in raising new improved varieties is still going on. Propagation is by division in spring or from seed.

L

**Lathyrus
odoratus**

Among popular garden flowers which have been
improved during the past fifty years or so, none have
made more striking advancement than Sweet Peas,
which have been greatly transformed since their
introduction to Britain nearly 280 years ago.

It was in 1699 that the Sweet Pea first came to
Britain, although it had been mentioned in literature
well before that time. It is a flower which both the
Greeks and Italians grew. In the earliest writings it
was referred to under several grand names, most of
which by present standards are both cumbersome
and unnecessary. For instance, one very early record
refers to the Sweet Pea under the title *Lathyrus disto-
palatyphylls hirsutis mollis magna et puramaeno flore odora-
tissimo purpureo*, which, of course, can be roughly translated as hairy, soft, of good size and sweetly scented.

It was not until towards the end of the seventeenth
century that literature and knowledge of the Sweet
Pea became at all widespread. The transformation of
the Sweet Pea really began with the efforts of a
devout monk named Franciscus Cupani in about
1695, when he was approximately twenty-four years
old. He was concerned with improving many plants,
but the Sweet Pea captured his real interest. It was
he who, in 1699, sent seeds of *Lathyrus odoratus* (the
name which was later standardised by him) to Dr
Uvedale of Enfield, Middlesex, with whom he
appears to have corresponded for some time. This
man, who was a schoolmaster, a keen gardener and a
botanist, is commemorated in the fruit world by the
Pear Uvedale's St Germain.

It is difficult to know precisely what the original
Sweet Pea was like. The oldest records seem to
indicate that it had two very small purplish flowers
on short stems. These were, however, produced in
great abundance and above all they had a most

pleasing perfume which, of course, is the origin of their common name. The first catalogue to offer Sweet Peas appears to have been that of John Mason of Fleet Street, London, who in 1793 offered five or six kinds including Painted Lady and one which he described as black. Early in the reign of Queen Victoria J. Carter, the founder of the famous seed firm of Carters Tested Seeds, offered a number of varieties including one which he called yellow. This description would appear to have been somewhat fanciful, since yellow is a colour which has not yet been produced and Sweet Pea breeders are still attempting to secure it. There are cream and sulphur varieties, but none that are really yellow.

The greatest improvement in Sweet Peas was, however, due to Henry Eckford. In 1870, when he was in charge of gardens at Gloucester, he saw a flower which was different from all the other plants in his care. He had a knowledge of plant breeding and had already improved a number of other subjects, but from this period he concentrated his efforts on Sweet Peas. He was most successful and it is true to say that the insignificant flower he found was developed into one of the most desirable of all annuals. He eliminated its weak points, improved the size and colour range of the flower, and, in spite of these improvements, he maintained and increased the perfume.

Subsequently many other people played a part in improving the Sweet Pea, but perhaps the next most important stage was the appearance of the type now known as Spencer Sweet Peas. This came about through the observance of Silas Cole, who was gardener at Aythorpe Hall, Northampton. He noticed on one plant that the standard or back petal instead of being plain was beautifully frilled. The flower exhibited in the Sweet Pea Show in 1901 was named Countess Spencer after Coles's employer's wife. Other growers found flowers with some frilling, but none as pronounced as that discovered by Mr Coles. Since this time many other improvements have been made in size, structure and colour. The National Sweet Pea Society is very active in promoting the Sweet Pea through its literature and shows.

Today we have such types as Multiflora, Galaxy, Jet Set, Knee-hi, Bijou and Cuthbertson's Cupid. None of these, however, have the same perfume as the older varieties, which fortunately can still be obtained in mixture that contains sorts such as Prima Donna, Dorothy Eckford and Lady Grisel Hamilton, all of which were popular sixty or seventy years ago. Although all of these are small-flowered and unfrilled, their scent and daintiness make them invaluable.

Reference to the catalogues of specialist growers from many parts of the world will disclose the wide range of colours available. Although there are now several cream varieties in cultivation, the long-awaited yellow seems as elusive as ever.

Sweet Peas are easy to grow. For preference, choose an open sunny position, if possible sheltered from north and east winds. Work the soil to a depth of about 35-38 cm (14-15 in) and add decayed manure, good compost and bone meal, placing these in the second spit and not near the surface. Do this early so that the weather breaks down the soil. Alternatively, seed can be sown in exactly the same way as for culinary peas. In sheltered positions, where the soil is well-drained outdoor sowings can be made during the first week in October and again in March. Seed can also be sown in pots in frames in October or in warmth from February onwards. Plants from indoor sowings have to be hardened off gradually before being planted outdoors in early April. Suitable supports should be given at an early stage.

Lavendula   The word lavender comes from the Latin *lava*,

meaning to wash, on account of its use in toilet water
and soap. The Ancient Egyptians used oil and plant
juices mixed with sand and Fuller's Earth,
sweetened with the fragrance of flowers, including
musk, to wash their bodies. In the first century it was
reported that Roman soap was composed of beech
wood ash and goats' fat.

In the time of Elizabeth I perfume was used
instead of soap, which having come from the
Continent, was still not widely available. Lavender
became an ingredient in soap at the time of Charles
I, who held the soap-making monopoly for England.
Being short of money, in 1671 he disposed of his
interest in soap to a merchant named William
Yardley. Yardley introduced lavender essence into
soap, which became so popular that Lavender plants
were specially grown for this purpose in many parts
of the country. It is still an important crop at
Mitcham, Surrey, the home of the Yardley firm, and
there are quite large areas of these plants grown in
various parts of Norfolk.

'Lavender', wrote Parkinson in 1629, 'is almost
wholly spent with us to perfume linen, apparel,
gloves, leather, and the dyed flowers to comfort and
dry up the moisture of a cold braine. It is put, with
other herbs, either into baths, ointments, or things
that one uses for cold causes.'

The soothing qualities of lavender seem to have
been well-known in olden times and even today they
are made use of by country folk, hence lavender
pillows and lavender tea – made by pouring a pint of
boiling water on a half an ounce of leaves. William
Turner in his *New Herbal*, dated 1551, stressed the
soothing quality of the herb when he wrote: 'I judge
the flowers of lavender quilted in a cap and daily
worne are good for all diseases of the head that come
of a cold-cause, for they comfort the braine very
well.'

Lavender was one of the ingredients used in the composition of the famous Four Thieves Vinegar, so its disinfecting qualities must have been appreciated even in the Middle Ages. Today country folk in Spain and France make a simple extract oil of lavender into a dressing for cuts and wounds. Lavender bags, applied hot, they use for relieving pain. In London 'Sweet Lavender' is the only one of the old street cries which still survives.

Lavender grows best in light soil which does not dry out in summer and the plants flower from July onwards. They should be pruned after flowering to keep them shapely.

There are a number of excellent species and varieties available including *Lavendula spica*, the Old English Lavender, which also has a white form, both growing up to 90 cm (36 in) high. From this have come a number of cultivars including Hidcote of dwarf compact habit, producing deep purple spikes, Munstead Dwarf, rich lavender-blue, and Twickel Purple. *Lavendula vera* is the Dutch Lavender, which has spikes of soft blue, the source of lavender oil.

Lilium

The Lily is a very ancient flower and we know from various records that it has been cultivated from the earliest days of civilisation. Reliable authorities tell us that many of the references to Lilies in the Bible refer not to the true Lily as we know it but probably to the anemone or iris. There is, however, a reference in the first Book of Kings to 'the chapiters upon the top of the pillars' in Solomon's temple being of Lilies. Lilies are also depicted in other carvings made many centuries ago. Although there seem to have been periods when Lilies were less popular, they have always been used for the decoration of churches and other places of worship. Among the kinds used for this purpose are *Lilium longiflorum* and *Lilium candidium*. The latter is best known under the name of the Madonna Lily and has for long been associated with the Virgin Mary, no doubt because of the purity of the white flowers, as well as because of their beauty and fragrance.

In an old *Herbal* of 1525 there appears to be the first mention in English of the Lily. It was more than another hundred years before Lilies were named, and then there were about twelve in cultivation. By the middle of the sixteenth century even more varieties were known. We can, therefore, be certain that Lilies have been grown in the gardens of the western world for well over four hundred years. Throughout this time the colour range has gradually widened. About one hundred years ago a number of books and other works on Lilies appeared, and these further popularised the plants. In addition, since 1932 the Royal Horticultural Society has arranged Lily Conferences and issued Lily Year Books.

From the end of the eighteenth century plant hunters were searching in many distant places for Lilies and other flowers. It was not, however, until about 1804 that the Tiger Lily became at all well-known. The first bulbs were sent to Kew from Japan and China, and, as soon as they flowered, they became an object of great interest. It is believed that this Lily was grown in China and Japan in large quantities over a thousand years ago. The name is derived from the Latin *tigris*, presumably on account of its colour, although tigers do not have purple spots!

The number of species and varieties available from many parts of the world is really tremendous. *Lilium auratum* is the Golden-Rayed Mountain Lily of Japan, which has been widely acclaimed as the queen of Lilies. Its white flowers are spotted red with a golden centre. This species appears to have been introduced to Europe from Japan in 1862 by the firm of Veitch, although there is evidence that it was grown in France in the seventeenth century.

Lilium brownii appears to be the name used for a number of Lilies, but the one now in general cultivation came from China and was sent to England by a missionary named Brown in 1935. It grows 1-1.3 m (3-4½ ft) high, carrying large funnel-shaped fragrant flowers of creamy-white, heavily shaded chocolate brown on the outside.

Lilium burbankii, created in 1900, is one of the many hybrids raised by Luther Burbank, the famous American hybridist, the colour of the true form being bright orange-yellow, flushed crimson towards the petal tips and spotted dark brown.

Lilium candidum is one of the oldest Lilies and can be found growing wild in southern Europe, Asia Minor and Palestine. Centuries ago the Madonna Lily was said to have had some value for healing wounds and curing internal disorders. It is said to have been grown near Roman camps to help keep the army fit. This species requires autumn planting, as opposed to the late winter and early spring planting of almost all other Lilies. There are a number of forms all with white flowers including one rare sort which has double flowers and another with variegated foliage.

Lilium dauricum is a native of north-east Asia, having been discovered in Siberia. It has upright reddish-scarlet flowers with brown spots.

Lilium davidii from China is named in honour of a French missionary-naturalist who first collected the bulbs nearly a century ago. It grows up to 2 m (6 ft) high and carries as many as twenty nodding orange-red flowers spotted black.

Lilium duchartrei from western China has been in cultivation since 1903. Brought to this country by the famous Richard Farrer, it was at one time known as the Marble Aartagon Lily.

Lilium hansonii is a particularly good martagon-type Lily from Korea. It first flowered in England in

1871 and now carries between six and twelve fragrant nodding, turk's-cap flowers on 1.3-1.6 m (4½-5 ft) stems.

Lilium henryii, a native of China, is very hardy. Its bright orange-yellow flowers, up to twenty of them, appear on 1.3-2.3 m (4½-7 ft) stems. Originally the bulbs were sent to Kew by Augustus Henry whose name they now bear.

Lilium leichtlinii commemorates Max Leichtlin, the famous German Lily specialist, who died in 1910. Introduced into Europe in 1867 this Lily is of Japanese origin.

Lilium pumilum with nodding scarlet flowers is a native of north-east Asia and was first grown in Europe about 1810. It is known as the Siberian Coral Crab and is also often listed as *Lilium tenuifolium* in reference to its slender 45 cm (18 in) stems and narrow grassy foliage.

Lilium regale was discovered by Dr E.H. Wilson in 1903. A native of West Swechwan in China, it was first grown by Messrs Veitch. It is said that in securing the original *Lilium regale*, Wilson injured a leg but thought it worthwhile to obtain such a treasure. A stem rooter, it should be planted not less than 12 cm (5 in) deep. The flower stems grow up 2 m (6 ft) high and these carry as many as two dozen funnel or trumpet-shaped, fragrant flowers. Each has a white mouth a sulphur-yellow throat and there are rose-purple stains on the outside.

Lilium speciosum introduced into Europe from Japan by John von Siebold, a Dutchman, in 1830 is of Japanese origin, and has beautifully spotted, white flowers.

Lilium superbum a native of the Eastern United States, has the common names of Turk's Cap Lily, Nodding Lily and Swamp Lily. Growing up to 2 m (6 ft) high, the stems carry orange flowers deepening to red toward the petal edges, with spotted centres.

Lilium szovitzianum. This name commemorates Nepomuk Szovits, an Hungarian apothecary, who died in 1830 and who is credited with its introduction. The canary-yellow flowers appear in June on stems varying from 60 cm-1.6 m (2-5 ft) high.

Lilium tigrinum came to England through William Kerr, a collector from Kew. The attractive red reflexed flowers aroused immediate admiration and it soon became popular and has remained so for many years.

Lilium wardii was discovered in Tibet in 1924, by the famous plant collector Captain Kingdon Ward. Its sharply reflexed petals vary from pale pink to a rich rosy-pink marked with purple. These scented flowers appear in July and August on 1.3-1.6 m (4½-5 ft) stems.

Through the work of hybridists including Miss Preston of Canada, R.O. Backhouse of Hereford, Jan de Graaff of the United States and many others there are now many marvellous hybrids available. We now have several groups of splendid hybrids including the Fiesta, Golden Chalice, Golden Clarion, Green Mountain and Olympic ranges.

Reference should be made to specialists catalogues regarding planting, since some Lilies are stem rooting. Many make excellent pot plants and practically all like a well drained, peaty loam and plenty of sun.

Lupinus
Better known as Lupins, the title of these plants comes from the world *lupus*, meaning 'the wolf', because the plants were once supposed to rob the soil of its fertility.

There are a number of Lupin species, among which are the following: *Lupinus albus*, the Levantine species, which has been cultivated since ancient times for soil improvement by digging in the plants while still small, and as a fodder crop. From July to September it produces white flowers on stems

45-60 cm (18-24 in) high.

Lupinus hartwegii, is the well known annual Lupin native of Mexico from which most annual Lupins have been developed. There are quite a number of colours, sometimes offered under separate names. These grow 45-60 cm (18-24 in) high.

Lupinus hirsutissimus from California, has hairy foliage and showy, rich rosy-red flowers. *Lupinus hirsutus* is the common blue Lupin of southern European origin. It is often grown as an agricultural plant, and has a white and red form.

Lupinus luteus is the fragrant yellow species, and may be used as a soil improver. *Lupinus pubescens* has soft hairy leaves and violet blue flowers marked white, which sometimes assume a purplish-red shade. *Lupinus tricolor* has whitish flowers changing to violet. This is reckoned to be of hybrid origin and is often in flower in early June. *Lupinus arboreus* is the Tree Lupin, which forms hard-stemmed bushy specimens usually with yellow flowers, although there is a white form.

Lupinus polyphyllus is the perennial Lupin so well known in the herbaceous border. It is from this species that the best of the modern varieties have come, including Downer's Delight and Blue Gown.

The most striking of all Lupins are those known as Russell Lupins which commemorate the work of George Russell (1857-1951). This man, who lived near Wolverhampton, spent more than a quarter of a century raising plants which he continued to hybridise until his aim to increase the size of the spike was accomplished. He first exhibited his treasures in 1937 at a show held in London by the Royal Horticultural Society. The plants were grown at the Boningdale nurseries of Messrs Baker of Codsall, Wolverhampton and during the first summer that they were shown, more than 70,000 people visited the floral farms at Boningdale.

The achievements of George Russell, who was then a man of 60 years old, had far exceeded his wildest dreams. He subsequently revealed that it was in 1911, when he first realised that there was some future in the Lupin if the old fashioned blue and white varieties could be infused with some varieties of colour. He began buying specimens of all the varieties he could, sending to many parts of the world for seed. He continued to cross and re-cross his seedlings, eliminating all but the very best, but it was not for ten years or more that he first saw real advance.

These new plants at once attracted attention and George Russell had many offers from various trade growers, offers which became more tempting as each year passed. However they were all refused because Russell realised that he had not yet achieved his object. It is said that one American enthusiast offered him 5 dollars for a thimbleful of seed, while other visitors to the trial ground were prepared to give as much as £50 for each particular plant, but still Russell had no intention of selling.

Even when he felt he had achieved all he had set out to do, he was not entirely concerned with the financial reward. He seemed more intent on ensuring that the plants he had raised should help to build up the career of a young man who had helped him for a number of years. When eventually he did dispose of his stock of plants, one of his conditions was that the young man was to be given the opportunity to continue to work among the plants that he knew so well.

Here indeed was a man who loved flowers, and put his best work into perfecting them, with such great success. The colour range is now tremendously wide, taking in tones of pink, orange, yellow, red and bi-colours such as purple and gold, apricot and sky blue, rose-pink and amethyst, and many other beautiful colour combinations. However Russell Lupins do not appear quite so long lived as the older *Lupinus polyphyllus* varieties.

All Lupins are best planted in spring and like good but not over-rich soil which is not too limy. They do best in a sunny position where their roots never dry out.

Propagation is by cuttings of new growth in spring or by division of the clumps. Excepting in a very few cases, Lupins do not come true from seed and vegetative propagation is the only way to ensure reproduction of particular varieties.

M

Matthiola

Many people, even some gardeners, would not recognise *matthiola* as the proper name of the plants usually referred to as Stocks. Botanically Stocks are very close to the Wallflowers, in fact, the common names of Gillyflower, Gillofre or Gillyvor have been applied to both these subjects.

Long ago to avoid confusion, the plants were divided and the word 'wall' was brought in to distinguish those which would grow on walls and 'stock' was reserved for those with hard stems. Matthiola commemorates the name of an Italian botanist and this family of plants is native to Western Europe. One species, *Matthiola incana*, the parent of the hardy biennial Brompton Stock, has its home in Great Britain.

All the classes of Stocks are well worth growing. These are the annual Ten Week, from *Matthiola annua*, which can be had in dwarf and tall strains, Brompton, Intermediate and the East Lothian.

Single Stocks lack the charm of the doubles but with several modern strains it is possible to select seedlings which will definitely produce double flowers. The procedure is to raise the seedlings in warmth and when they are about 12 mm (½ in) high, move them to a temperature of 8-10°C for two or three days. Some seedlings will then have dark green leaves and these should be discarded, for the lighter foliage indicates plants that will produce double flowers.

The Ten Week strain should be sown in warmth in spring for bedding out in May and June. The Bromptons are sown in summer for flowering the following year, while the Intermediates including the East Lothians, can be sown in a frame in August and be potted up for greenhouse culture for blooming in winter and spring.

The hardy annual *Matthiola bicornis* is known as the Night Scented Stock, its lilac-coloured flowers emitting a sweet fragrance in the evening. During daylight, the flowers are closed and the plants look bedraggled.

Wallflowers in spring and Stocks in summer, give us the same delicious scents as enjoyed by the gardeners of the Elizabethan period, but with large blooms, richer colours and more double flowers.

Myosotis The ancient story of the accidental drowning of a young man who in his last despairing appeal to his lover threw her a flower as he asked her not to forget him, has given this plant its popular name of Forget-Me-Not. It is not on sentiment alone that the myosotis is a popular garden flower for it has much to commend it. Perhaps it is fitting that one of the species is named *palustris* indicating it likes marshy or wet soil, in fact, all Forget-Me-Nots do best where the ground remains moist.

There are a number of good species available, all flowering in summer. These include *Myosotis alpestris*, blue and white. This has many forms growing 15-18 cm (6-7 in) high, some being fragrant. Among the best are Marine, 15 cm (6 in), the dwarf plants

being covered with bright blue flowers; Carmine
King, 30 cm (12 in) has deep rosy-carmine flowers
on erect stems and Royal Blue 30 cm (12 in), is a rich
indigo-blue. A white form is sometimes available,
but often the flowers are faintly stained lilac or pink.

Myosotis azorica, 15-19 cm (6-7½ in), is blue and
Myosotis sylvatica, 30-60 cm (12-24 in), is a tall-
growing blue species native to Britain.

Even newer varieties are in the course of being
perfected, one of the aims being to secure plants
which are of compact habit. All are essentially
flowers of the spring, for they begin to look tired in
the summer.

Although plants can be divided, Forget-Me-Nots
are so easily propagated that it is not worth keeping
old plants. Seed can be sown in fine soil on a cool site
in May or June, and the seedlings put in their
flowering quarters by October.

These plants will succeed in pots and with a little
careful, gentle forcing will flower in winter.

N

Narcissus

The exact date of origin of the narcissus, including
the trumpet varieties often referred to as Daffodils, is
unknown, although it is mentioned by Gerard in
1597. Other authors who published books many
years before Gerard also refer to this cultivated
flower, which grew in other countries besides our
own.

This genus is generally held to have been named
after the youth in the Greek legend who was changed
into this flower. The youth rejected the love of the
nymph, Echo. To punish him, Nemesis made him
fall in love with his own image reflected in a fountain
– like the narcissus which seems to gaze down at its
reflection as it grows beside the water. Some

authorities assert however that the word narcissus is derived from the Greek *narke* or torpor, from whence comes our word narcotic. Be this as it may, the narcissus has featured in poetry for centuries.

Narcissus really came into their own at the time of the special conference in 1884. This was a conference arranged to confirm the systematic order of all known varieties, after which Mr Hartland of Cork published the first catalogue entirely devoted to Daffodils. During the next twelve months Peter Barr, a famous plant collector, listed systematically all the known varieties and his firm, in conjunction with F.W. Burbidge, published a booklet entitled '*Ye Narcissus a daffodyl flowre and hys roots with hys culture*'.

Daffodils are actually a section of the narcissus family, and are usually defined as those varieties which have a trumpet as opposed to the short cups, crowns or corona of those varieties normally identified as narcissus.

Much hybridising throughout the years has resulted in a certain amount of confusion with regard to the sections of the genus. Until toward the end of the last century, there were three main groups known as *Magni-coronati*, corresponding roughly to the trumpets, *Medio-coronati*, being those with cup-shaped crowns, and *Parvi-coronati*, those with small, saucer-like centres. The R.H.S. subsequently had the entire genus divided into ten sections: *Narcissus trumpet*; *Narcissus imcomparabilis*; *Narcissus barrii*; *Narcissus leedsii*; *Narcissus triandrus* hybrids; *Narcissus cyclamineus* hybrids; *Narcissus jonquilla* hybrids; *Narcissus tazetta*; *Narcissus poeticus* and various. Some years ago, however, a further alteration was made, these names were dropped and the ten divisions reclassified as: (1) trumpets; (2) large-cupped; (3) small-cupped; (4) double; (5) triandrus; (6) cyclamineus; (7) jonquilla; (8) poetaz; (9) poeticus and (10) species.

The triandrus hybrids are dwarf-growing, with pointed trumpets and reflexed petals, ideal for pot and rock garden work. Cyclamineus hybrids are small-flowering, with narrow, attractive, sharply reflexed petals. Many species deserve mention, but they too, will be found detailed in modern bulb catalogues. One of the most unusual is *Narcissus viridiflora*, which produces its greenish flowers in November and December, before the foliage.

The Daffodil grows in various European countries including Scandinavia, Spain and the Balkans. The name daffodil is said to be a corruption of Asphodel the lovely flower that grew in the Elysian fields.

The first description of the Daffodil to be published in English, was by William Turner who had premises near the present site of Kew Gardens, in the early part of the sixteenth century. Then, there were only a few varieties, but the famous John Parkinson attached to the Court of James I, took up the cultivation of the Daffodil and soon a number of species were found and many varieties introduced. In one of his records he describes the plants as the Nonesuch, the cup resembling the chalice that is sometimes used to hold the sacramental wine.

Famous names connected with the development of the Daffodil include: John Rea; William Herbert, who was Dean of Manchester Cathedral; John Horsfield, a weaver in the North of England who was keen on hybridising; and Edward Leeds, a stockbroker. In the nineteenth century Peter Barr did much to increase knowledge of, and interest in, the modern Daffodil. Apart from his own introductions he subsequently came into possession of the special varieties secured by William Backhouse and Edward Leeds. He travelled widely, seeking to collect all the wild species he could. One of his great achievements was the re-discovery of *Narcissus cyclamineus* which had been lost for many years.

One of the most striking advances in the story of the Daffodil occurred in 1911. At the Investiture of the then Prince of Wales, the Daffodil was officially adopted as the National flower of Wales. Before that time it seemed uncertain whether the leek or the Daffodil was the national emblem. Centuries ago when the English overran Wales, loyalists could identify themselves by picking either a leek or a Daffodil or in fact any similar plant, so long as it had a green stem which was white at the bottom. Both leeks and Daffodils were in common cultivation in the countryside of Wales during the time of Henry Tudor.

Narcissus benefit from early planting, and August and early September are good times for outdoor culture although bulbs can be planted until November. Cover the bulbs with at least 10 cm (4 in) of soil. Many narcissus in all sections can be grown in pots or bowls: start them under cool conditions so that a good root system develops before there is much top growth.

Nerine

The name nerine comes from 'Nereid': the Nereid were sea nymphs, the fifty daughters of Nereus a sea-god. These plants, of which many flower before the foliage develops, are remarkable for their showy autumn colour, each petal appearing to be liberally dotted with golden dust in the sunlight.

The story of the introduction of *Nerine sarniensis* is of great interest being associated with many legends and theories. At one time there was much rivalry between the Dutch and the English for the mastery of the seas and, since in both countries flowers of various kinds were greatly valued, Dutch and British mariners sought plants in South Africa, among other places. The Cape flora is of course one of the richest in the whole world and it is probable that the wreck of a ship known as 'Haarlem' in the middle of the seventeenth century was instrumental in bringing to light many subjects which had not previously been well known. It is said that the shipwrecked crew had to camp for some months in the area which is now Cape Town, and they were able to grow various crops there. Subsequently, settlers from the Dutch East India Company arrived and with them several gardeners who were needed to grow food crops for the colony. These gardeners were able to collect various South African flowers which were to prove of interest and value in their native lands.

Records show that ships engaged in East India trade carried the bulbs and plants that had been collected by these first colonists of South Africa. In 1655 one of these Dutch ships was wrecked in the English Channel and among the debris washed ashore were a number of bulbs which landed on the island of Guernsey. It appears that they remained buried in the sand until autumn came and the action of the wind and waves revealed the bulbs, but more than that, these bulbs produced their showy red and pink flowers in great abundance.

Fortunately the climate of Guernsey suited these bulbs, which were subsequently identified as nerines. They were grown for cut flower purposes for market sale. This proved to be a great success and the many shades of colour which eventually appeared made them even more popular, so much so that, at one time, demand greatly exceeded supply.

First referred to as lilies they were not really identified as nerines until some time later, when they were found to be growing naturally on the rocky slopes of the Table Mountains and were then identified as *Nerine sarniensis*.

This subject is now widely grown and known as the Guernsey Lily although, of course, it is only because of the way in which the bulbs were found that it has any claim to such a title.

There are numerous species and named hybrids

available today in many attractive colours. The bulbs flourish in well drained pots of sandy loam, decayed manure and leaf mould and flower from early July until November, often before the leaves appear. They require a winter night temperature of not less than 8-10°C. The foliage remains green until April or May when the bulbs should be allowed to rest.

O

Oenothera

The name comes from two Greek words: *oinus* meaning wine and *thera* meaning eager pursuit, and is an old title given by Theophrastus. At one time the roots were said to be eaten to provoke a relish for wine.

Oenothera biennis is a biennial often known as the Evening Primrose and it was introduced to Britain from the U.S.A. early in the seventeenth century. It escaped into the wild and is now usually regarded as a member of both the British and American flora. It can be found in varying forms growing to as much as 2 m (6 ft) high, on sand dunes and other semi-wild places in various parts of the country.

Both roots and leaves have been used as a vegetable in the United States, France and, during the 1939-45 war, in Germany. Medicinally, this plant is said to have curative properties for breathing troubles such as asthma and whooping cough.

There are a number of perennial oenotheras of herbaceous or shrubby habit, some being of prostrate growth, others growing up to 1 m (3 ft) high. *Oenothera fruticosa* is a golden-yellow, day-flowering species which has a number of named forms. *Oenothera speciosa* is a choice sub-shrubby plant having white tinted, pink, fragrant flowers on 60 cm (24 in) stems.

All grow in well cultivated sandy soil and prefer a sunny situation. Propagation is by seed, division, or in the case of the perennials, by cuttings.

P

Paeonia

This names comes from Paian the surname of Apollo the God of Healing. John Parkinson in his famous work in 1629 wrote 'the paeonies give fresh pleasure every year without further trouble and they certainly flower freely once established.'

It is believed that the old double Paeony was introduced to Britain during the time of the Crusades. The plant was devoid of scent although the double crimson flowers were of good appearance. It was the introduction of *Paeonia lactiflora*, towards the end of the eighteenth century, that brought perfume to Paeonies. This is a white flowered single species having several forms, all being heavily scented and was discovered in Siberia by a Russian traveller who, it is said, found that roots were being eaten in the same way as potatoes, while a diffusion of seeds made a pleasing drink.

Early in the nineteenth century Paeonies were grown at Kew Gardens but we are indebted to the French for the introduction of many of the charming varieties in cultivation today. *Paeonia officinalis* was used as the main parent, the other parent being one of various Chinese species. The varieties resulting were a selection of first class plants all bearing scented flowers, some of which, together with their decendents, are still found in present day catalogues.

Lemoine, the famous French firm, introduced varieties such as Madame Crousse with scented pink flowers, while Duchesse de Nemours an excellent highly scented red variety, also came from France about 1856.

James Kelway of Langport, Somerset was a great specialist of 90 years ago. Many of his *Paeonia officinalis* varieties are still available. His selection of single Paeonies with their conspicuous and sweet fragrance was outstanding: one of his earliest varieties, the lilac tinted Lady Veronica Bruce, appeared in 1887. He concentrated on perfume and produced many with conspicuous golden stamens.

Paeonies do not like to be disturbed and rarely flower the first season after being moved. They do well in deep, moist ground rich in compost and containing lime. Plant in October or very early spring and a mulching of old manure in spring leads to good flower development.

Papaver
This is the proper name of the plant we know as Poppy. The title comes from the Latin world *Pappa* – milky juice.

Papaver orientale, an excellent perennial plant, is sometimes known as the Eastern Poppy and originated in Eastern Europe in the borders of Persia and Afghanistan. It has been grown in Britain since the beginning of the eighteenth century.

Before this time, the blood-red *Papaver bracteatum* was imported from Siberia in 1817. This species is recommended by many as being the best garden plant of the two: the flowers not only appear earlier but they last longer.

It was, however, Amos Perry, the well known plantsman of Enfield, who between 60 and 70 years ago, began experimenting with these Poppies in order to raise better varieties. He achieved considerable success and some of his plants were given the R.H.S. Award of Merit. His original successes produced flowers of red and white, but it was the plants which carried flowers in shades of pink that pleased him most. One which is still much in favour was named Mrs Perry, which has handsome apricot-pink flowers.

5. *Papaver rhoes – the Poppy*

Other breeders were successful in raising different coloured varieties and there were improvements in the firmness of the stem as well as the colour range. Perry's White is another famous sort which has been grown for over 50 years. Other varieties which are still widely grown and valued, include: Lady Haig, glowing scarlet; Marcus Perry, orange-red with black central blotch and May Sadler, salmon and shrimp-pink.

Although oriental poppies are ideal for the herbaceous border they are of little value as cut flowers since they do not last well. They flourish in ordinary good soil which does not dry out in summer.

Papaver nudicaule is the Iceland Poppy with orange-red flowers. Hybridists have now produced a whole range of varieties in many art shades.

Papaver rhoes. Shirley Poppies are now greatly valued and they have come to us as the result of the observations and diligence of the Rev W. Wilkes of

Shirley in Surrey. In the summer of 1880 Mr Wilkes saw one flower in a batch of the Corn Poppy, *Papaver rhoes*, which differed from all the others in that the margins of the petals were lined with white. This plant he marked and carefully saved the seed. The next season he had several hundreds of seedlings, of which only a few showed any real difference from the ordinary Corn Poppies. For a number of years Mr Wilkes selected all seedlings which showed any real signs of variation and in due course he developed the now well known strain of Shirley Poppies that can be depended upon to come true from seed.

The modern Shirley Poppies have silky petals and a tremendously wide colour range taking in shades of rose, salmon-pink, crimson, orange-scarlet and smoky tones. None of these have the typical black central blotch of the wild English Poppy, but they are dependable showy annuals growing 45-60 cm (18-24 in) high and flowering freely from July to October.

Other forms of the Shirley Poppy include: Ranunculus flowered, beautifully shaped; Begonia flowered, a double strain in mixed colours, and Carnation flowered, another distinct type in a wide colour range.

Papaver somniferum is the Opium Poppy, an annual from which the seeds were used to make the drug.

All can be sown in spring where they are to flower for they do not transplant well. Seed can also be sown in a sheltered place in September for very early flowering.

Pelargonium The pelargonium or geranium has been in cultivation for well over 300 years. Some consideration should be given as to exactly which plant we are referring, since the connection between the names geranium and pelargonium causes considerable confusion.

The name 'geranium' has its origin in antiquity,

having been used by Dioscorides, who lived in the days of Nero and Pliny. The name, as defined by Linnaeus in his Species Plantarum of 1753, comprised three distinct genera: geranium proper or Crane's Bill; pelargonium or Stork's Bill and erodium or Heron's Bill. These names are descriptive of the shape of the seed pods. The genera pelargonium and erodium were created by a French botanist L'Heritier, in 1788. The true geranium is a cosmopolitan genus of which about eight species are native of South Africa. It is seldom cultivated as an ornamental garden plant in South Africa, although a number of introduced species, and a few species of erodium as well, occur as weeds.

Pelargoniums are distinguished from geraniums by their irregular flowers, by the nectariferous spur which adheres to the pedicel, and by the shape of the fruit.

Pelargonium, though largely South African in origin, extends to Madagascar and up to the east coast of Africa to Arabia and western India. There are species in Australia and on Tristan da Cunha. From the South African species have arisen all the manifold varieties of pelargonium and so-called 'ivy-leaved and zonal geraniums' of horticulture.

Some botanical writers of the early nineteenth century insisted on following the usage of Linnaeus, and declined to accept the new name pelargonium. Among these was H.C. Andrews who in the preface to his monumental work on the geranium, published about 1820, says: 'If such generic divisions, that is the splitting of Linnaeus's genus into geranium, erodium and pelargonium were generally adopted, the approach to botanic science would be so choked up with ill-shaped, useless lumber that, like a castle in a fairy tale, guarded by hideous dwarfs, none but a botanic Quixote would attempt to investigate'. The genus pelargonium is accepted by botanists today.

Among the hardy plants which were collected by early visitors to the Cape, and which survived the voyage to Europe, was *Pelargonium triste*, a humble plant of the sandy flats and lower slopes. It is a low growing, rather inconspicuous plant, which attracts little attention from modern gardeners.

Thomas Johnson in his edition of Gerard's herbal published in 1633 refers to it as follows: 'There is of late brought into his kingdome, and to our knowledge by the industry of Mr John Tradescant, another more rare and no less beautiful than any of the former, hee had it by the name of Geranium indicum noctu ordoratum; this hath not as yet been written of by any that I know; therefore I will give you the description thereof. The leaves are larger, being almost a foot long, composed of sundry little leaves of an unequal bigness, set upon a thick and stiff middle rib and these leaves are much divided and cut in . . . they are thicke, green and somewhat hairie; the stalks is thicke and some cubit high; at the top of each branch upon foot stalkes some inch long, grows some eleven or twelve floures, and each of the floures consisteth of five round pointed leaves of a yellowish colour with a large blacke-purple spot in the middle of each leafe as it were painted, which gives the floure a great deal of beauty; and it also hath a good smell. I did see it in floure about the end of July 1632 being the first time that it floured with the owner thereof. We may fitly call it Sweet Indian Storkbill or painted Storksbill, and in Latin Geranium indicum odoratum flore maculato'.

The inclusion of the word *indicum* shows that, as with a number of other Cape plants taken to Europe by ships returning from the East, *Pelargonium triste* was thought to come from India or the Indies. John Tradescant's garden was in Lambeth, South London.

In 1635 Parkinson wrote of *Pelargonium triste*: 'The

flowers smell very sweete like Muske in the night
onely and not at all in the day time as refusing the
Sunnes influence but delighteth in the Moones
appearance'.

During the eighteenth century many pelargoniums found their way into the European gardens.
Among these was *Pelargonium inquinans* which was
one of the forerunners of many types of red
geraniums. It is said to have been cultivated as early
as 1714 by the then Bishop of London. The
forerunner of the Ivy Leaved geranium, *Pelargonium
peltatum*, was introduced to Holland in the year 1700
and from that time it has been developed so that we
now have many first class named sorts.

The Show or Regal pelargonium is *Pelargonium
domesticum*, which in America is known as Martha or
Lady Washington. There are, of course, many
scented pelargonium species such as *Pelargonium
citrisdorum* and *Pelargonium crispum*.

With the great and revived interest in all members
of the pelargonium family, large numbers of new
varieties including many handsome variegated
forms have been produced during recent years.

There are a number of fragrant leaved species
including those with rose, citron, lemon, nutmeg and
other scents. Many of these have elegantly cut
foliage.

As the result of intensive hybridisation a number
of other groups of pelargoniums have been raised.
These include Cactus, Poinsettia, Bird's Egg and
Dwarf strains. Undoubtedly the most widely grown
of all are the *Pelargonium zonale* varieties which are
now available in so many pleasing colours. The
scarlet variety Paul Crampel was once the best
known, but reference to the catalogues of specialists
growers will reveal the existence of scores of named
sorts in many art shades and plain colours.

Phlox   The name phlox comes from 'flame' and alludes to the brilliant colour of the flowers. The plant has been grown in gardens for several centuries but is modern when compared to many old favourites which have been linked with the lives of very many generations of plant growers.

There is evidence that in Elizabethan days perennial phlox were known only as a weed in the wilds of North America and Siberia, and they lack the legends surrounding many of our most loved plants.

The parentage of the modern phlox is through *Phlox paniculata* and *Phlox maculata*, or *decussata* as it is sometimes referred to, the latter having purple flowers and often regarded as late flowering. All the plants in this group like sun and a moist, but not wet, root run and produce their flowers in panicles or clusters. They are available in many named varieties in a wide colour range. All have one great enemy – eelworm – which works from within the stems and eventually kills the plants.

There are a few early flowering perennial phlox, usually referred to as belonging to the *Phlox suffruticosa* group, although some are *Phlox divaricata* varieties.

Phlox subulata, purple, is dwarf growing and excellent for the rock garden since it rarely grows more than 15 cm (6 in) high. It has various named varieties in a good colour range.

The annual *Phlox drummondii*, purple, grows about 30 cm (12 in) high. Introduced from Texas in 1855, it has various forms known as cuspidata (pointed); fimbriata (fringed); grandiflora (large); flore-pleno (double) and nana compacta (dwarf and compact). A modern strain of the latter is Twinkle Dwarf Star, 15-18 cm (6-7 in) producing a showy mixture of gay colours.

Propagation is by division or cuttings for the perennials and by seed for the annuals. If the latter are sown in warmth in early spring and the plants are hardened off before being placed outdoors in May or early June, they will flower throughout the summer.

Primula   These are harbingers of spring. The name itself comes from *primus* – the first, an allusion to the earliness of the flowers. The family takes in many favourite subjects: *Primula auricula*; *Primula officinalis* (or *veris*) – the Cowslip; *Primula elatior*, the Oxlip and *Primula vulgaris* (*acaulis*) which is the Primrose.

The polyanthus is an hybrid between the Primrose and Cowslip both of which are British native plants. Hybridists have done a great work in producing the many selections now available. These include the American bred Pacific Giants which have flowers up to 7 cm (3 in) in diameter. Apart from the mixtures, they can be had separately in blue and other shades. A fairly new introduction is Greensleeves of which the flowers come in shades of pale green, lime-green and creamy-green, so eminently suitable for many indoor floral decorations.

The gold laced polyanthus are the most striking and are likely to have been secured by crossing red polyanthus with a natural hybrid, *Primula pubescens*, well over two hundred years ago. The sweet scented flowers have a gold centre as well as gold edging which shows up so well against the main crimson or maroon ground colour. At one time there was great rivalry on the show bench where these polyanthus were exhibited but now the gold laced variety is quite scarce. Quite hardy and apart from growing outdoors, they make excellent pot plants, while when cut and placed indoors in vases, the flowers last a long time in good condition, usually scenting the room with a honeysuckle-like perfume.

Polyanthus are among the longest flowering spring plants. Germination of seeds is slow but new season's seed, sown in June in boxes or pans and kept in a cool shady place, usually brings good results although seed can also be sown in prepared beds in the open.

Apart from separate colours there are several unusual types of polyanthus which include the Munstead Strain, a selection of the lighter colours, and the new F.1 hybrid strain Crescendo Formula Mixed, in which hybrid vigour has given strong, healthy uniform plants with grand flowers.

Common names include Galligaskins or Jack on the Green in which each floret is surrounded by a green leaflet and Hose-in-Hose in which each flower has another within it.

Primula vulgaris, once known as *Primula acaulis* is the common Primrose and a form once distributed as *Primula altaica* is now recognised as *Primula v.var rubra*. Of easy culture, its requirements in soil and situation must be obvious to all who have seen the primrose growing wild in Great Britain and elsewhere. There are various sub-species including *Primula v. balearica* from Majorca which is almost snow-white and sweetly scented. *Primula v. ingwersiana* found in Greece in 1929, is also white, with downy leaves. Separate slightly varying forms of the so-called English primrose are to be found in Pembrokeshire and Durham as well as in such Mediterranean areas as Turkey, Greece, Persia, Switzerland and the Caucasus.

Primroses retain their foliage throughout the year and withstand the cold, soon bursting into flower, after being held in the grip of frosts.

There are many other species of primula including those for moist situations such as *Primula pulverulata* Bartley Strain, pink and red, and *Primula japonica*, red and *Primula florindae*, yellow; all on 60 cm (24 in) stems. *Primula denticulata* is excellent for the rock garden or front of the border. This has narrow crinkly leaves and clusters of pale lilac to blue-mauve flowers on short, stout stems. In addition, there are species of Primroses ideal for greenhouse or living room including *Primula obconica*, *Primula malacoides* and *Primula stellata*.

Primula auricula

Best known as the auricula and sometimes as the Mountain Cowslip this plant has been grown in European countries for centuries. It has been known at various times as *Primula* or *Auricula ursi* and more familiarly as Bears Ears, the latter probably because of the shape of the leaves and the hairs or farina appear on them.

At one time, it seems that the roots of the plants were thought to have some medicinal value. Many of the older varieties had flowers of striking colours some being conspicuously edged with a contrasting colour, while a black auricula was a highly prized plant. Another striking feature of these older varieties was the size of the flower truss, some being composed of several dozen pips or separate flowers.

The auricula belongs to the mountainous regions of Europe and found its way into this country towards the end of the sixteenth century by way of Holland and Belgium, being introduced by the Flemish Weavers who came to this country fleeing from religious persecution. These people settled in various parts of the country and particularly on the borders of Lancashire and Yorkshire where they carried on their work and handed down to the next generation their love and knowledge of the culture of the auricula. They were also responsible for introducing the gooseberry.

The auricula became very popular and was grown to such an extent during the eighteenth century that it was found in nearly every garden in the northern counties. It was eagerly sought after by every gardener and so a Northern Society was founded for the cultivation of this flower.

The enthusiasm for this plant began to penetrate

to the southern counties and a conference of gentlemen interested in the advancement of horticulture was held at South Kensington on November 8th 1876 when the following resolution, amongst others, was unanimously agreed to: 'To hold an exhibition of auriculas in London in 1877 and that the gentlemen present do form a committee with power to add to their number to carry out the same'.

At a meeting held on December 6th 1876, it was reported that the Crystal Palace authorities would make arrangements to hold an Auricula show on April 24th 1877. The first show was eventually held as planned at the Crystal Palace and was later published as 'Grandest display of these interesting old-fashioned flowers which has ever been held in London or elsewhere.'

Today the auricula is still popular and there are grey, white and green edged varieties in cultivation. Several societies are devoted to the cultivation and publicising of the auricula, which can still be had in many named varieties, some with smooth leaves, others thickly covered with white powder.

Auriculas grow well in partial shade and like a fairly heavy loam with rotted manure and leaf mould. Propagation is by detaching offsets in summer or from seed in the case of mixed varieties.

Primula veris   This is the Cowslip, one of the best loved of native British flowers. The common name is derived from an Old Saxon word 'cuslippe', since at one time, it was thought by some country folk that the fragrance of the flowers was like that of a cow's breath.

Many years ago the chopped flowers were mixed with tea, as this was said to improve the flavour. Cowslip wine is still thought of as a desirable drink, while the leaves were once used in salads.

The Cowslip has been much used in hybridising and has influenced the appearance of the polyanthus as well as the Oxlip, the latter being the result of the mating of the Primrose and the Cowslip and possibly other hardy Primulas.

The plants are of compact habit with attractive greyish-green leaves and rich yellow flowers. Although they seem to be unobtainable now, a few years ago it was possible to secure seed of some splendid mixed hybrids on 30 cm (12 in) stems, taking in shades of bronze, biscuit, gold and reddish-crimson.

Seed can be sown as soon as ripe either in boxes from which seedlings can be transplanted or direct to flowering positions. Grow the plants where there is plenty of humus matter in the soil. This helps to hold moisture and encourage a good fibrous root system, which will do much to keep the foliage in good conditions and aid flowering.

Pulsatilla vulgaris

It is believed the Romans brought *Pulsatilla vulgaris* to Britain where it can still be found growing wild in isolated places.

For many years known and catalogued as *Anemone pulsatilla*, this is a most lovely flower producing cups of opalescent colour in spring. As the sepals expand, they reveal a golden filigree ball of pollen-laden stamens and a finely tasseled brush of anthers. In dull weather and at night, the sepals close and become enveloped in silken threads.

Often known as the *Passe Fleur*, an early French name for the anemone, the name became pasque in the writings of Gerarde and others. This was thought to be related to the word 'Pasch', the Jewish Passover. Later the plant became associated with Easter and it is certainly true that flowers open at around the annual Easter season.

There are several good forms in cultivation, including Mrs Van der Elst and Red Clock, both being a reddish-blue colour and Budapest variety, purple-blue.

Other pulsatillas include *Pulsatilla alpina*, a native of the high meadows of the European Alps where it produces clusters of stems each bearing a solitary white flower with pink or blue shading on the back of the sepals. A form known as *sulphurea*, 30-40 cm (12-16 in), is somewhat difficult to grow. In early spring its furry buds unfold to disclose clear sulphur-yellow flowers.

Pulsatilla pratensis 40-60 cm (16-24 in), has rich wine coloured petals with purple stigmas and golden stamens. *Pulsatilla vernalis* is one of the most beautiful of all. If it is provided with a congenial situation where the roots can work their way into enriched moisture-holding humus matter, it will produce sturdy buds, protected with filigree leaves and golden hairs, which unfold to show the delicately tinted white flowers. The thick fleshy roots must not be damaged or they may decay. They can be raised from seed provided it is fresh.

In Gerard's herbal we are told 'the Passe Floure hath fine jagged leaves, closely couched together which resemble an Holy-water sprinckle . . . In Cambridgeshire where they grow, they are named Coventrie bels.'

All like moist peaty soil and a semi-shaded situation.

Q

Quamoclit

Belonging to that large convolvulus family this name comes from two Greek words, *kyamos* – kidney and *klitos* – dwarf. Sometimes known as the Cypress Vines, the quamoclits are now usually grouped with the calonyctions and pharbites and often catalogued under the name of ipomoea.

Among the 400 or 500 species are some which need greenhouse treatment, many which are quite hardy, some evergreen and others deciduous. Many climb or twine and should not be confused with the Bindweed or Convolvulus which is such a troublesome weed.

They come from widely separated parts of the world, mostly from warm climates some extending into North America.

Quamoclit or *Ipomoea Bona-nox* from tropical America, was introduced to cultivation in 1773. Its white flowers in July and August appear towards eventide, hence the epithet *bona-nox* – good night.

Ipomoea jalapa has red, white or pinkish-purple flowers. Half hardy, it is said that the tuberous roots have been known to weigh more than 40 lbs. *Ipomoea pandurata* is the wild Sweet Potato Vine from North America and *Ipomoea batatas* the well known Sweet Potato, which has edible tubers.

Quamoclit nil is a half hardy annual producing light blue flowers from July to September. Often listed as *Ipomoea hederacea* it is a native of tropical regions and a resin known as Pharbetisin and used in medicine is obtained from the seed of this plant. *Ipomoea quamoclit* produces solitary red flowers throughout the summer.

Quamoclit rubro-coerulea, usually catalogued as ipomoea having pinkish-blue flowers, came into cultivation in 1830. From this have come the many varieties we know so well as Morning Glories. These include Wedding Bells mauve, Flying Saucers blue and white and Early Call Rose with rose flowers having a white throat and as much as 10-11 cm (4-4½ in) wide.

The perennials can be propagated by taking cuttings of short shoots in spring and inserting them in peaty soils in bottom heat. Alternatively, layers are usually easy to root.

The annuals can be raised from seed sown in warmth in March and April.

R

Reseda odorata   This is the Latin name of the popular plant known as Mignonette, which is said to be a fragrant weed of ancient Egyptian gardens. It appears to have come to Britain about the middle of the eighteenth century, having previously reached France, probably from the gardens of North Africa. It was actually the French who gave the plant its common name of Mignonette, which literally means 'little darling', a term which identifies plants referred to at various times as the Fragrant Weed, or the Frenchman's Darling.

Mignonette is a plant once grown on the balconies of houses in London, and other cities, since its perfume in hot summers helped to blot out the odours arising from the narrow streets, where cleanliness and health were of little consequence. Some people thought that the scent of the flowers gave protection from diseases too, and certainly Mignonette was once believed to have power to ease bodily disorders, for the Latin meaning of the name is to heal or assuage. It is recorded that seeds were used by the Romans as a sedative.

Until the beginning of this century, Mignonette was widely grown as a pot plant in the British Isles. From that time too, it became cultivated as a garden subject, and new named varieties were introduced.

Mignonette has long been a florist's flower for including in bouquets and decorations. Culture is easy: for pots, sow thinly directly into the pots, thinning the seedlings to three or four per pot. Indoor sowings can be made in succession from early March until September and, outside, from the end of April onwards, where the plants are to bloom. Select a position where the soil has been broken down finely and sow thinly. Modern fragrant varieties include *Reseda luteola*, greenish-yellow, Goliath, red and Red

Monarch, a particularly lovely red and green flowering cultivar.

Rosa

The earliest history of the Rose is shrouded in mystery. No one knows exactly how old it is, but it is certain from the fossils of Roses found in various parts of Asia, Europe and America that many thousands of years have passed since the first bushes were to be found growing wild. There is evidence that many of the earlier species had very few petals.

A large number of species are now in cultivation many of which we sometimes class as shrub Roses. *Rosa canina*, the Dog Rose, is often to be found in hedgerows. *Rosa gallica* (Rose of Provens) the French Rose, is still in demand as are the Damask Roses and *Rosa chinensis* the China Rose, through which has come the Old Crimson, a favourite variety of years ago.

As a result of pollenation and selection the so-called hybrid perpetuals were developed, although few of these are cultivated today. They were mostly scentless.

The so-called Tea Roses developed from *Rosa odorata* and *Rosa gigantea*, and not only were they continuous flowering, but the colours were delicate and the perfume delightful. They were not quite so hardy as the perpetuals with which they were eventually crossed to produce the now widely grown hybrid Tea varieties.

Rosa bifera was once known as the Monthly Rose because it flowered more continuously that the older China Rose. *Rosa rubra* is the Red Rose of Lancaster, a species through which many of our garden Roses have evolved.

Rosa damascena is the old Damask Rose noted for its patterned, fragrant flowers. There are summer and autumn flowering forms, one of the former being the famous York and Lancaster, pink striped Rose. *Rosa centifolia* is the old Cabbage or Provence Rose, sometimes known as the 'Rose of a hundred leaves'. A favourite with the old master painters, the slender flower stalks bear lovely fragrant, double pink flowers. It has numerous named forms including de Meaux with tiny, flat double pink blooms and La Noblesse sweetly scented, pink. *Rosa centifolia muscosa* is the Moss Rose of which there are many forms, including Crimson Moss, crimson-shaded maroon and William Lobb, a vigorous grower with rich purple-magenta flowers fading to lilac-grey.

Rosa eglanteria (*Rosa rubignosa*) is the Sweet Briar having many fragrant single pink flowers on thorny stems of 2 to 3 m (6-9 ft) high. Among the many varieties, there is a group known as the Penzance hybrid Sweet Briars growing up to 2.40 m (7½ ft) high. These include Amy Robsart, deep rose; Lady Penzance, coppery-salmon, and Meg Merilees, single, rosy-crimson. *Rosa foetida* is the Austrian Briar parent of many of our modern yellow Roses.

Rosa hugonis is a ferny Chinese Rose made more beautiful by its numerous cupped, soft yellow single blooms in May. The hybrid Musk Roses have come from crosses between *Rosa moschata* and various modern varieties. In June and July, many sweet musk-scented flowers are produced. Bushes grow 1.8-2 m (5½-6 ft) high, little pruning being needed. Good varieties include: Danae, creamy-yellow; Felicia, fragrant silvery pink to salmon; Penelope, salmon-cream-pink and Will Scarlet, vigorous growing with strongly scented red flowers.

Rosa bourboniana. The Bourbon Roses are hybrids between *Rosa chinensis* and *Rosa damascena*. Famous varieties include: Boule de Neige, with glossy foliage and creamy-white flowers in summer and autumn; Gruss an Teplitz, crimson; Louise Odier, camellia-like pinkish-lilac; Mmme Pierre Oger, creamy-blush rose and Zéphirine Drouhin, thornless, with scented cerise-pink flowers.

The old hybrid perpetual Roses are well worth growing but not easy to obtain. They include: Hugh Dickson, a large fragrant red variety; La France, silvery-pink; Mrs John Laing, well shaped 'full' soft pink; Prince Camille de Rohan, dark velvety crimson and Ulrich Brunner, a vigorous pillar Rose introduced in 1882. This has fragrant, blowsy, double, large cupped, rosy-lilac-pink flowers.

Rosa banksaiae is a white flowered species introduced from China in 1807. *Rosa rugosa* came from Japan in 1845. It has large red flowers and rough leaves and there are a number of forms with flowers in varying colours all of which are followed by large brilliant fruits or hips.

Rosa moschata has been grown since Elizabethan days. Its single fragrant cream flowers appear on vigorous climbing stems. There are several named varieties as well as hybrids. *Rosa noisettiana* is a hybrid between *Rosa moschata* and *Rosa chinensis*. Varieties which include Gloire de Dijon, and Marechal Niel, have been famous for well over one hundred years.

Rosa spinosissima is the Burnet or Scotch Rose, notable for its black hips. Many hybrids are now available including Fruhlingsmorgen, a most exquisite single pink Rose with black stamens and hips.

The Wichuriana Roses, originating in Japan, are excellent for pillars or posts as well as for clothing banks. A particularly good variety is Francois Juranville, with glossy foliage and salmon pink flowers.

Rosa willmottiae makes a small graceful shrub with grey-green leaves and small rosy-mauve flowers.

So we come to the modern varieties of Roses so widely grown today. There are many successful British raisers including: Cants of Colchester; Gregory, Stapleford; Le Grice, North Walsham; Wheatcroft of Nottingham; Harkness of Hitchin; Cocker of Aberdeen; Hicks of Reading and MacGredy of Portadown. Specialist raisers abroad include the firms of Meilland and Pernet-Ducher of France and Kordes of Germany, and we cannot ignore the work of American raisers who have done much to improve the hybrid Tea Roses. These are renowned for their elegantly shaped blooms, usually produced singly, occasionally in clusters. Many have a wonderful fragrance and according to variety, grow up to a metre high, making them ideal for beds and borders.

New bush and climbing varieties are introduced annually while some drop out of cultivation, often due to lack of demand rather than faults. The hybrid Teas have shapely high pointed blooms of good quality. They are freely produced with usually, a most pronounced fragrance. They are excellent for exhibition and some will withstand quite severe disbudding.

The early hybrid Teas owe their origin to crosses between the Tea Rose and hybrid perpetuals with a certain amount of back crossing. These were followed by the Polyantha-Pompom type which came into being about 100 years ago. The first two hybrid Polyantha Roses were raised in Denmark in 1924 by crossing a Polyantha-Pompom variety with hybrid Teas. These were named Else Poulsen and Karen Poulsen. Since that time very many varieties have been raised and the group name has become Floribunda instead of Polyantha.

Continued crossing has resulted in the term Floribunda-Tea type since the flowers though smaller, are carried in clusters sometimes produced on quite tall stems.

The ancestry of many of the best known of today's varieties can be found in the catalogues of specialist Rose growers.

S

Sprekelia formosissima

This plant has acquired a host of common names including the Aztec Lily, Jacobean Lily and the St James' Lily, the latter ostensibly because the perianth segments resemble the red cross embroidered on the cloaks of the Knights of St James of Calatrova.

The sprekelia genus, which has one species only, stems from Mexico and Guatemala, and is named after J.H. von Sprekelsen, an eighteenth century citizen of Hamburg whose fine garden and botanical library brought the famous Linnaeus to his door. Whenever these flowering plants are seen they create much interest. Their elegant, distinctive appearance makes it seem unlikely that they can be improved, even with modern hybridising systems.

The large, oval, long-necked bulbs are sheathed in black tunics and produce several long, deep green strap-like leaves and one or two 45-60 cm (18-24 in) pink floral stems, crowned with a single, glorious and vivid crimson-scarlet flower. The striking and decorative flowers have six petals with a curiously orchid-like appearance. The slim upper petals are held erect while the lower ones partially enclose the stamens. The leaves usually appear at the same time as the flowers but sometimes the flowers appear before the foliage.

The Jacobean Lily, as it is known in Britain, used to be cultivated in greenhouses only, but it adapts itself to sheltered gardens in the south and west. Cultivation is simple: the bulbs should be planted shallowly in well drained soil with plenty of organic matter, in congenial positions towards the end of April. The fascinating flowers appear in June or July. Lift the bulbs in the autumn before frosts come and store in a dry, temperate place during the winter. One to three bulbs can also be planted in pots from February onwards, making sure that a third of the bulb remains above the soil. Little water is required for the first ten days but when growth begins, increase the water supply. If kept in the light in a warm room indoors, the bulbs develop quickly and produce their magnificent, long-lasting red flowers in March and April.

When grown in pots, sprekelia should be watered and 'liquineured' after flowering until the leaves turn yellow, then lay the pots on their sides to allow them to dry off for a ripening and resting period.

T

Tagetes

This title is derived from a mythical Etruscan deity and is the official name of the plants we normally refer to as African and French Marigolds which are quite distinct from the well known Pot Marigolds, of which the Latin name is Calendula.

These common names are a little confusing since tagetes originate from the American continent, although they are now widely grown in all parts of the world. Some attempts have been made to make tagetes the national flower emblem of the U.S.A.

In Spain, Marigolds were once favourite flowers to place on the altar of the Virgin Mary. For this reason the plants and flowers became known as Mary's Gold. In India, these flowers have some religious significance and it was in that country that the Marigold first became known as the Friendship Flower.

The tagetes family consists of more than 20 species including *Tagetes erecta*, the African Marigold; *Tagetes patula*, the French Marigold and *Tagetes tenuifolium* which is the true species having varieties such as Golden Gem. All are natives of Mexico and are showy summer flowering plants with pungent foliage.

For centuries writers have lauded these plants particularly the African Marigold, described by Parkinson as 'a plant of grace and glory'. The last 40 years have seen remarkable development in the breeding of tagetes many of which have become first class favourites with exhibitors.

As a result of detailed breeding programmes, we now have dozens of choice varieties, the F.1 hybrids being particularly good. Of the double French hybrids, Honeycomb, 25 cm (10 in), bronze-red gold edged; Seven Star Red, 30 cm (12 in), mahogany-red, and Sparky, 25 cm (10 in), red and gold, are outstanding. Single varieties include Cinnabar, 25 cm (10 in), mahogany, and Dainty Marietta, golden-yellow, maroon blotches. The African F.1 hybrids produce a prolonged display and include Appolo, 35 cm (13 in), with large orange flowers and Diamond Jubilee, 60 cm (24 in), double yellow.

A fairly new strain known as Odorless Mixed, 80 cm (32 in), produces double Carnation-like blooms 10 cm (4 in) in diameter. Absence of foliage odour makes this mixture suitable for cutting.

Seed of all tagetes should be sown in boxes or pans of fine soil during March or April, the seedlings being hardened off for planting outdoors in May or June. Seed can also be sown in the open ground in early May for a later display.

Tulipa   The Tulip was unknown in Western Europe before the middle of the sixteenth century. There is no mention of such a flower in any of the earlier lists of plants, or in general literature, and it is hardly likely that so attractive a flower would have escaped notice. When the Tulip was introduced from Turkey, it was hailed by all the botanists and gardeners of the time as a great innovation. The testimony of many writers indicate that the Tulip grew wild in the Levant and was thence brought from there to

Britain. Tulips were also found near Constantinople, in various parts of Syria, in Arabia, Macedonia and the Crimea.

It is interesting to know that many of those found in our gardens have been propagated from the species named after Conrad Gesner, who first made the Tulip known by a botanical description and a drawing. He tells us that he first saw it, in the beginning of April 1599, at Augsburg, in the gardens of the learned Counsellor John Henry Herwart. The seeds had been brought from Constantinople or, according to others, from Cappadocia. These had produced a large, single beautiful red flower, like a red lily. It had a very sweet, soft and subtle scent. Wild Tulips have been known in southern Europe for centuries including *Tulipa australis* and *Tulipa kaufmanniana* which grow freely in Algeria, Morocco and Spain.

The first reference to the Tulip is contained in a letter written by the Ambassador of the Emperor Ferdinand I at the Court of the Sultan of Turkey. Journeying near Constantinople, an abundance of Tulips which the Turks called 'tulipan', was everywhere offered to him.

After the Tulip became known, Dutch merchants and rich people in Vienna, began to order them from Constantinople. According to the Dutch writer Hakluyt, the first bulbs planted in England were sent from Vienna about the end of the sixteenth century.

These flowers, which have no use save to ornament gardens, which are exceeded in beauty by many other plants, and which are of short duration, became, in the middle of the seventeenth century, the object of a trade unparalleled in the history of commerce – their price rose above that of the most precious metals. This trade was in the main confined to certain towns in the Netherlands, notably

Amsterdam, Haarlem, Utrecht, Alkmaar, Leiden, Rotherdam and Enkhuizen, and rose to its greatest heights in the years 1634-1637.

Henry Munting, a learned botanist, recorded at the time a few of the prices then paid. For a single bulb of a variety called The Viceroy, the following articles were agreed to be delivered: 2 tons of wheat, 4 tons of beer, 2 tons of rye, 2 tons of butter, 4 fat oxen, 1,000 lbs of cheese, 3 fat pigs, 12 fat sheep, 2 hogsheads of wine, a complete bed and a suit of clothes.

Later on, Tulips were sold according to the weight of the bulbs. 400 perits (a perit is a small weight less than a grain) of Admiral Liefhen cost 4,400 florins; Semper Augustus was often sold for 2,000 florins. Wassenaer, in 1623, writes that the latter was the variety of the year, and it seems to have maintained its reputation for a long time. From a drawing in the Krelage collection, it was a variety with long narrow petals, scarlet on a white ground. Munting recounts that at the height of the Tulip mania, in 1636, one bulb of Semper Augustus was sold for 5,500 Dutch florins (then about £460) and another for 4,600 florins, together with a new carriage and two horses. Another man agreed to give twelve acres of land for one bulb. Those who had no ready money promised their movable and immovable goods – houses and land, cattle and clothes. A man whom Munting once knew won by his trade more than 60,000 florins in the course of four months.

One merchant gave a herring to a sailor, who had brought him some goods. The sailor, seeing some valuable tulip bulbs lying about, took them to be onions and ate them with his herring. Through his mistake, the sailor's breakfast cost the merchant a much greater sum than if he had entertained the Prince of Orange!

The trade in bulbs was not only taken up by

mercantile people but also by noblemen and citizens of every description: seamen, farmers, turf diggers, chimney-sweeps, footmen, maid servants etc. At first, everyone won and no one lost. Some of the poorest people gained houses, coaches and horses in a few months. In every town a tavern was appointed as a 'change' where high and low traded in bulbs. They made laws to their own advantage and had their own notaries and clerks. The trade became a pure gamble, in which bulbs were sold, and resold for profit, while still in the ground. An early crash was inevitable, when there was so little real value behind it all, and this came at the end of 1636, when all holders tried to dispose of their bulbs. The Tulip mania had excited an interest altogether out of proportion with the true situation. Indeed, no new development took place; nothing exceptional had happened; the whole affair grew out of a passion for speculation.

In England, the fancy grew during the nineteenth century and reached its height between 1830 and 1850. High prices were paid, as much as £100 and £150 being received for one bulb.

Then as the flowers came within the reach of all classes they ceased to be grown for their rarity, or as objects for their owners to show off, but were cherished for their own sake. The commencement of the nineteenth century heralded a new period in the history of bulb culture. Hitherto, the amateurs' one desire had been to possess the greatest number of varieties of a particular kind of flower and to show these off to their friends. Little importance was attached to colour harmony or tasteful grouping, and this applied especially to Tulips.

As far as the gardener of today is concerned the Tulip family is divided into a number of large sections, each one containing varieties with distinctive characteristics. These sections can easily be found in the catalogue of any specialist bulb grower. They include the types of Tulip which are seen at their best in the rock garden. The Early Single and Early Double varieties bloom from March onwards.

The stately Darwin varieties are at their best in April being followed by the Triumph, Mendel and Rembrandt or broken varieties. The latter are sometimes classed as Bizarres or Bybloemens according to their parentage. After these come the Cottage, Breeder, Parrot and Lily Flowered varieties.

Tulip bulbs like deep planting in autumn. They should be covered with at least 10 cm (4 in) of soil, with more if the soil is very light.

U

Ursinia

This is an attractive genus of half-hardy annual or perennial herbs and shrubs which are natives of South Africa although one or two also come from Abyssinia. Named after John Ursinus of Regensburg who lived from 1608 to 1666 this family includes plants sometimes known as sphenogyne.

Unlike many South African Daisies, the flowers remain open throughout the day and with their graceful foliage, they make very ornamental plants. *Ursinia anethoides* was once known as an arctotis. It has finely cut foliage and wiry stems up to 30 cm (12 in) high carrying rich orange-yellow flowers each with a purplish central zone.

Ursinia dentata has toothed coppery petals on curved stems. *Ursinia pulchra* is a really handsome annual producing, on 15-30 cm (6-12 in) stems, showy rich orange flowers with a black zone which appear from July to September. For best results these plants should be grown in well drained soil, in a sunny position.

Sow the seeds thinly in trays or boxes in the cool greenhouse and gradually harden the seedlings before planting them in the open ground in early June. Ursinias make marvellous pot plants for the greenhouse while they can be used as temporary house plants.

V

Viola odorata

Over two thousand years ago the ancient Greeks chose the purple sweet Violet to be the symbol of the city of Athens. Records show that it was then possible to cultivate plants so that flowers could be gathered throughout the year. This was important, for no Greek ceremony was complete without the traditional garland of Violets.

The culture of the plant dates from ancient times. The Persians in AD 204 translated an old Aramaic manuscript on the cultivation of Violets, and in Turkey and Syria the flowers were used in the making of sherbet, the national drink. Greek and Roman herbalists believed that insomnia could be cured by a compress of Violets. This is very pleasant indeed, but only for a short time, as the substance ionine (which gives Violets their perfume) deadens the sense of smell of most people and after a few inhalations the flowers seem to become scentless.

Apart from its ornamental value, it was also valued for its seeds for, with those of the strawberry, Poppy and other subjects, they were once used as a remedy for headaches and similar troubles. Violet flowers were also said to be good for curing inflamation of the lungs and alleviating hoarseness and thirst. Centuries ago too, they were said to have had some powerful influence against evil spirits.

These ancient Violets were particularly valued because of their scent, and it was said on many occasions that of all the fragrant herbs, none could compare with that of the purple Violet. This perhaps is why some of the best known varieties carry the titles of Princess of Wales, Czar and Rosina.

6. Viola – the Pansy

The so called wild species *Viola odorata*, can be found growing in shady places not only in England, but in Himalayan districts and also in the shady gorges of some of the Mediterranean regions where the soil has a high leaf mould content. *Viola canina* the wild scentless Violet is also a native of many countries.

We must not forget the Parma Violet, for although little is known regarding its origin, it seems likely that it first grew in some Moorish garden in Spain, although there are also evidences of it growing in Turkey and Italy. There are many legends associated with this tiny flower which is such a world wide favourite. Wordsworth summed this up concisely when he wrote: 'Long as there are violets, they shall have a place in story'.

Perhaps it was the love of the Empress Josephine for flowers that made the Parma Violet famous and it is said that the Empress included Violets in her wedding bouquet.

Napoleon too, valued them and when he was banished from France his last words were 'I shall return with the Violets in the spring'. It is said that after the death of Josephine Napoleon visited her grave and picked some Violets growing there, keeping them near his breast until his death.

Violets also appealed to Shakespeare, Chaucer and Milton whose writings include many references to these sweet scented flowers.

While it is difficult to trace the exact parentage of modern Pansies and Violas, we do know that Pansies have sprung from Viola tricolor. The name pansy is a corruption of *pensêe*, the French word for thought. Other common names are Heartsease, Love-in-Idleness, Jump up and Kiss Me, Tickle my Fancy and Three-Faces-under-a-Hood.

Pansies can be said to be British plants since they grow well in the United Kingdom as well as Ireland and the Channel Islands.

Work on improving the Pansy has been going on for a very long time. Great advances have been made in size, form and colour and there are various fancy strains now available. These have a strong ground colour surrounded by a band of a contrasting shade, producing a gay effect.

There are show Pansies having brownish-purple blotches laced with yellow and crimson with upper petals showing lemon-yellow and purplish-crimson. Famous strains which are not now generally available include Empress, Masterpiece, and Trimadeau.

There are also strains without the whisker marks and these are usually referred to as the Clear Crystals strain.

As garden plants, the bedding Pansies can be most effective when grown of their own, while they are ideal as edging plants and for window boxes. They are also excellent for pots and for exhibiting.

By its literature and Shows, the National Pansy and Viola Society maintains the interest in this old fashioned yet modern plant.

Violas or Tufted Pansies have long been popular. They are of hybrid origin, some of the Garden Pansies having been used as parents. While it is sometimes difficult to distinguish between Garden Pansies and Violas, there is a great difference between the Exhibition Fancy Pansies and Violas. The latter produce more flowers although the blooms are usually smaller. Though small, the plants have the qualities of abundant flowers and brilliant colour, producing bright effects over a long period.

There is a range of charming miniature Violas known as Violettas in many lovely colours, freely produced on compact plants. Violas are one of the few old, widely grown plants that have no common name, but this does not mean they have been ignored or slighted.

Gerard says of Violets and Violas 'there be made of them garlands for the head, nosegaies and posies, delightful to look on and to smell . . . Gardens receive by these, the greatest ornament of chiefest beautie and gallant grace . . . they do bring to a liberal and gentlemanly mind . . . honestie comelinesse and all kinds of vertues'.

Violets flourish in soil containing plenty of organic matter. They are first class for frame culture where the flowers can be produced well in advance of the open ground flowering period. The finest varieties are rarely grown from seed, but are propagated by runners, cuttings or division, which is best done in spring.

Named varieties of Violas and Violettas are also propagated by cuttings, although there are some first class mixtures now available including those known as Herald and Bambini. Pansies too, can be propagated by cuttings of named sorts including F.1 hybrids such as Sunny Boy Yellow, Imperial Blue and Imperial Orange or seed in the case of mixtures.

Veratrum   This is an ancient plant having the common names of False or White Hellebore. The Latin name is one used by Pliny and Lucretius and literally means 'truly black' referring to the colour of the root.

There are about ten species of these hardy perennial herbs coming from Europe, North America and Russian Asia. The thick rhizomatous roots are poisonous as are the root fibres. It is from the roots of *Veratrum album* that a powder is prepared and used for destroying caterpillars.

Veratrum album growing up to 1.5 m (5 ft) comes from widely separated European countries and was first known in 1548. The large panicles of whitish-green flowers show in July. A form known as *Veratrum a. viride*, from North America, has greenish flowers. *Veratrum maackii* from Eastern Siberia, has been known in cultivation since 1883. Throughout the summer the dark purplish flowers appear in loose panicles up to 30 cm (12 in) long.

All species flourish in fairly rich soil and are easy to grow. Propagation is from seed or by careful division.

Viscum album   Popularly known as Mistletoe and always attractive, the question of how it arises and flourishes was something of a problem for early botanists.

Gerard wrote of it as, 'an excrescence which hath not any root, neither doth encrease himself of his seed as some have supposed; but it rather cometh of a certain moisture gathered upon the boughs and joints of trees, through the barke whereof this vaperous moisture proceeding bringeth forth the Mistletoe.'

We, today, know better than our ancestors. We have long realised that Mistletoe is an evergreen parasite plant reproduced from seed encased in its sticky berries when lodged in the bark of apple, pear, hawthorn, or other trees – probably by birds. It is easily grown and cultivated.

It is said by some old writers that because Mistletoe was not allowed to decorate Christian churches, it was given a place in the kitchens of ancient manor houses and stately homes. There it hung with its white berries shining; and when a maid was found standing beneath it, any young man present had the right to claim a kiss and pick a berry from the bough with each kiss taken.

There seems to have been one exception to the exclusion of Mistletoe from Christmas decorations in churches. Old records reveal the fact that on the eve of Christmas Day, Mistletoe was carried to the high altar of York Cathedral and laid there as a relic of Druidism. The Druids, it seems, at Yule-tide took Mistletoe in their hands – they called the plant 'all-heal' – and laid it on their altars 'as an emblem of the salutiferous advent of the Messiah.'

The Druids cut the Mistletoe, with great cere-mony and ritual from the oak which they held to be sacred. They believed that this parasite plant grew on the oak in order to take care of the spirit of the great tree which, to them, seemed temporarily dead in winter. As a matter of fact, Mistletoe seldom grows on the oak, preferring those trees with soft bark such as the apple, the pear and the hawthorn. It is wonderful how its thread-like root pierces the bark and is able to fix itself firmly in the growing wood from which it takes the juices best fitted to sustain its life. Being a true parasite it derives nourishment from its host, never from the soil, or from decayed bark.

The Mistletoe figures largely in legend. In Brittany, where it grows abundantly, it is known as Herbe de la Croix because, so it is said there, the cross on which Christ suffered was made of its wood. For this reason, legend has it, the Mistletoe was degraded and became a parasite. The Druids believed that the Mistletoe protected its owner from all evil and their priests vouched for wonderful cures effected by the plant. For a long time it was prescribed as a cure for epilepsy and even in recent years, especially in France, Mistletoe pills were given as a remedy for high blood pressure. The powdered leaves, berries and twigs are used to make medicine and prepared as a fluid extract, taken in very small doses. Bird-lime has been made from the berries – I say has been, because one hopes that in these days bird-lime is only mentioned as a thing of the past!

Shakespeare, writing of the 'baleful mistletoe,' is referring to the Scandinavian legend in which blind Hoder, god of darkness, shot and killed Balder, the Apollo of the North. Being restored to life, the Mistletoe was presented by Balder to the Goddess of Love and everyone that passed under it was given a kiss to show that love and not hate was the Mistletoe's emblem.

The old Christmas carol, 'The Mistletoe Bough,' also has a strange story behind it. It refers to the daughter of Lord Lovell, famous in gardening history for his interest in and experiments with 'things botanical'. His daughter, Lady Agnes, took part in a game of hide-and-seek in which Mistletoe was used to add an extra dimension to the fun. She hid herself and although she was sought for everywhere no trace of her could be found. It was not until many years later that her skeleton was discovered in an old, oak chest. It seems that poor girl had been unable to lift the heavy lid of the chest once she had hidden herself inside it.

There are more than 400 known species of the Mistletoe – the larger number tropical, and some have showy flowers. The only British species is the Common Mistletoe (*Viscum album*).Thrushes are fond of the berries, and for this reason the 'Missel' thrush is said to have been given its name.

W

Watsonia

Named in honour of William Watson a Chelsea botanist or chemist who lived from 1715 to 1787. Often known as the Bugle Lily, this is a handsome plant related to the gladiolus with similar corms and sword-shaped leaves.

Natives of South Africa, they produce in June spikes of tubular flowers which sometimes give the appearance of crocuses on a stem. As the result of many years of growing in the more temperate regions, watsonias are no less hardy than gladiolus. In the past, there has been some confusion regarding the species, some of which have been classed as antholyzas or merianas. This uncertainty has been overcome and the following species are true watsonias all belonging to the natural order *Irideae*: *Watsonia augustifolia* delicate rose-pink flowers on 1-1.2 m (3-4 ft) stems; *Watsonia meriana* (Madam Merian's) terra-cotta; *Watsonia ardernei*, white and *Watsonia rosea* (pyramidalis) mauvish-pink on stems of 1½ m (4½ ft).

All flourish in sandy peaty soil where there is plenty of moisture during the growing season. November is a good time to plant in pots for greenhouse work, but do not plant outdoors until March.

X

Xeranthemum This name comes from *Xeros* – dry and *anthemon* – a blossom, alluding to the dry nature of the flowers which retain their colour and form for years. This is why they are used as immortelles or 'everlasting' flowers. A very old name for this hardy erect branching annual was Harrisonia.

Natives of Mediterranean districts and of the Orient, there has been some doubt about the identity of a few of the species some of which are now grouped with the helichrysums or helipterums.

A considerable interest exists regarding the use of everlasting flowers but the xeranthemums are among the most reliable. There should soon be newer species available but in the meantime, *Xeranthemum annum* is one of the best, its purple flower heads appearing in July.

Culture is of the simplest: seeds can be sown outdoors in April and a light covering of rich soil is all that is needed to encourage the plants to grow and flower well.

Y

Yucca The origin of this name is uncertain but may have some connection with Wanihot or Iucca, a plant from which tapioca and other edible matter is obtained. Certainly Indians once used the fibres of Silk Grass for making clothes as well as yucca cordage.

It is not immediately obvious that this plant belongs to the noble family of the Lilies. They are natives of Central America, the Southern United States and Mexico. Even so, many of the thirty or so species, all with narrow pointed leaves, tolerate, and even thrive in European climates. As long as 150 years ago there were six or seven species offered in the catalogues of British nurserymen, particularly in the list of Messrs Backhouse of York.

Yuccas are quite ancient plants and were mentioned in Gerard's herbal as long ago as 1593. There is reason to believe that plants flowered in British gardens more than three hundred years ago.

It is evident that this plant is much hardier than was originally thought, although flowering does seem to be rather erratic at times. Certainly in the early seventeenth century it was only rarely that the blooms appeared and when they did so they caused some excitement.

Yacca gloriosa, having the common name of Adam's Needle, Spanish Bayonet and Mound Lily, was one of the first introduced to general cultivation. This is the species with cream flowers often to be seen growing along the promenades of seaside towns.

Yucca filamentosa is perhaps, more reliable for blooming at a younger age. It is sometimes known as Silk Grass the specific name being given because of the curly threads that hang from the leaf margins. It has a variegated form.

Yucca glauca and *Yacca flaccida* (smaller growing) have been known since 1813, and *Yucca recurvifolia* came to notice about 1795. This is one of the best, having graceful dark green narrow leaves nearly 60 cm (24 in) long and greenish-white flowers on 90 cm (36 in) stems during August and September. Fruit is very occasionally produced. In the case of *Yucca gloriosa* it is of cucumber-like appearance, and a purple colour but very bitter to the taste.

All yuccas have sharp spiny leaves and need handling with care.

Z

Zea maize

Coming from Mexico and better known as Sweet Corn, there are various new and unusual strains available. These include Rainbow or Variegated popcorn, of which the seed in the cob or ears is multi-coloured. Apart from its edible value, this is a splendid decorative variety. There is also a Tom Thumb form of this coloured strain. Other oddities in sweet corn are Black Clarage and Black Tom Thumb, Red Tom Thumb, Purple Husk, and Gingham of which the seed is blue, purple and white, just like an old-fashioned gingham dress.

A warm, well drained, but moist, enriched situation should be chosen for this crop. While the seeds can be sown in the open at the end of May, it is best to raise them under glass, sowing in pots of compost or in soil blocks. Transplant when danger of frost has past, spacing them 30 cm (12 in) apart in a little block, rather than in one long row. This helps with the pollination process. Pinch out the side shoots. 'Tassels' develop at the top of the stems; these are the male flowers. Lower down are the silks or female flowers on which the pollen must fall to fertilise them. The seeds which form in the cob pass first through a watery stage, then a milk stage, which is when they should be gathered. Afterwards they become doughy and hard, when they are more suitable for poultry food.

Zea Mays everta is a type of Sweet Corn which is sometimes used for popcorn. Here again, there are different varieties. In the United States of America, popcorn is quite a large industry. To grow corn for 'popping' the cobs are allowed to mature instead of being gathered at the milky stage. Next the papery sheath is removed and the cob dried thoroughly. The grains can then be rubbed out easily. Thorough

Zinnia

drying is essential for popping corn. To prepare the grains, drop them into a small saucepan containing a layer of margarine or lard. After a few minutes over a low flame, the grains will pop. Then they can be served with sugar or salt.

The home of the zinnia is Mexico. The flower was named in honour of Dr J.G. Zinn, professor of medicine at Gròttingen, Hanover.

Few annual plants have been more improved during the last half century than the zinnia. Skilful work by hybridists has brought about a subject having not only a very wide colour range, but one greatly diverse in the size of plant and flower.

Interesting and attractive types include the Dwarf or Pumila varieties growing 30 cm (12 in) high, the Pompons, Scabious and Picotee flowered, the Cactus type, and the Dahlia flowered section, which grow 1-1.3 m (3-4 ft) high and produce very large blooms, frequently 15 cm (6 in) in diameter.

The Peppermint Stick is an exciting striped form of zinnia developed by the famed zinnia specialists, Bodgers of California. This strain brings a galaxy of vivid colour combinations, carmine and white, pink and white, scarlet and white, orange and yellow, red and yellow, etc., and approximately 70% of the flowers are striped. Peppermint Stick can be a fascinating surprise as some flowers come up with colours divided half and half or quartered and they are ideal for unusual flower arrangements. It is one of the cut-and-come again zinnias, and the blooms will continue until frost, if kept picked.

The particular strains from which Peppermint Stick has been developed, have an unusual story, that can be traced back to about one hundred years ago, when the handsome Archduke Maxmillian of Austria, and his attractive bride, Carlotta, were selected by Napoleon III to reign as the Emperor and Empress of Mexico.

This couple made their colourful entry into Mexico City where a vast crowd had assembled and bells rang out joyfully. Both felt the responsibility of this great adventure and Carlotta studied Spanish and took pains to learn the legends, customs and traditions of Mexico. She fell in love with the flowers and under her direction the gardens of the Palace blossomed with colour. One of her favourites was the little *Zinnia elegans*. In one of her letters she wrote 'this brilliant Flower of the Sun (zinnia), is always colourful, but these seeds I am sending you for your garden are of a most unusual kind that has striped petals'. It was not the custom for royalty to indulge in gardening, but Carlotta was a home lover as well as an Empress. Maxmillian and Carlotta soon discovered that they had been deceived, many factions opposed their reign and they were deposed. Perhaps the only fruits of Maxmillian and Carlotta's brief reign in Mexico were the flower seeds that Carlotta sent to Italy and Austria.

Lovers of floral history long wondered what became of 'The Flower of the Sun' with 'striped petals', about which the Empress Carlotta had written so enthusiastically. It seemed to have vanished until shortly after the First World War, when breeding stock from southern Europe was received in America. This discovery started a long and persevering effort of selection and re-selection. Just prior to the Second World War, a zinnia was selected that was beginning to take on the appearance of Peppermint Rock, although the percentage of striped flowers was small. When the 1939-45 War brought an interruption in extensive flower seed growing, the best stock was preserved in hermetically sealed cans, until hybridists resumed experiments. In 1950, Peppermint Stick was brought to its present brilliance and abundant striping, and seeds were released in 1951. Interest was phenomenal, and the demand quickly exhausted the small quantity available.

Persian Carpet is another variety. This is different from all other forms, being a most dainty miniature derived from *Zinnia augustifolia*. Introduced to Europe by a German plant explorer about one hundred years ago, *Zinnia augustifolia* which is also known as *Zinnia haageana* and *Zinnia mexicana*, was grown by many of the larger European seed houses and became a favourite in the later nineteenth century. In Victorian times, this small zinnia was prized by species-conscious Englishman. There was not much choice of colour in the original *Zinnia augustifolia*, and it passed from favour, being all but forgotten until hybridists produced Persian Carpet, with its deep colours and pointed petals edged with contrasting tones.

In endeavouring to improve the little *Zinnia augustifolia* and thereby return it to favour, hybridists brought about distinct 'breaks' some years ago. From here on it was a matter of continuous refining to produce the rich colourings of Persian Carpet, well deserving of the common name of 'cut and come again'. An even later development is *Zinnia Thumbelina*. Growing 15 cm (6 in) high, the colours include white, yellow, lavender, pink, orange and scarlet.

Zinnias are half hardy annuals which need to be sown in warmth in March or early April. The seedlings should be gradually hardened off for planting outdoors from the end of May according to soil and weather conditions.

Section Three

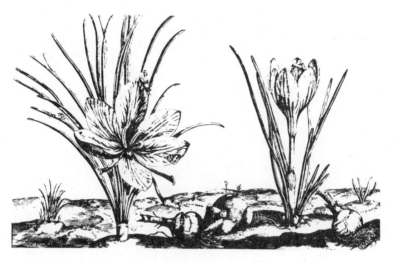

7. Crocus

Generic Names

The way in which plants are named has always created interest. It is done most scientifically and over the years the system has been brought to near-perfection. Certainly, there is now more evidence of the way in which plants are related than was once the case.

It was Linnaeus, the Swedish botanist, who proposed a system of classification based on the make-up, including the sex organs, of plants. Since his time, nearly two hundred years ago, Linnaeus's system has been modified, while other systems have been advanced. This means that as knowledge increases the status of some species and of some genera may alter.

Among the many families in the flora of the world are the following, which here we can only mention without giving descriptive details that in any case can be found in writings on botanical classification.

Amaryllidaeae The amaryllis family also contains many popular bulbous subjects. In many cases they are similar to their lily 'cousins.' Some have rhizomatous or fibrous roots. Included are: amaryllis, alstroemeria, crinum, galanthus, narcissus and nerine.

Araceae Another large family of decorative plants some of which bear fruit. Included are arums, anthuriums, acorus, dieffenbachia, monstera and philodendron.

Araliaceae Many members of the ivy family have attractive foliage. Among them are aralia, panax, dizygotheca, fatsia and hedera.

Bromeliaceae   The pineapple family contains both ornamental and food producing species, among which are ananas, bilbergia, cryptanthus and vriesia.

Cactaceae   The cactus family takes in many genera and species of greatly differing habit of growth and appearance. They are mostly grown in greenhouses where they produce a really colourful display. Included are cereus, opuntia, nyctocereus and pereskia.

Campanulaceae   The bellflower family accounts for campanula, platycodon, phyteuma and specularia.

Caryophyllaceae   The best known in this group are dianthus (including carnations), gypsophila, lychnis, sagina and silene.

Cistacea   Although a small family, the rock roses, consisting of cistus and helianthemum, are most attractive.

Compositae   This is the daisy family which includes various plants used for edible purposes including lettuce, chicory and scorzonera. There are many separate groups within this family all arranged according to their botanical make up. Among their number are heliathus, aster, helenium, calendula, senecio and anthemis, all containing different varieties.

Crassulaceae   Members in this family include sempervivum, crassula, echeveria, kalanchoe and sedum.

Cruciferae   Often known as the crucifer family this takes in a very wide range of well known plants including some vegetables such as the brassicas and mustard and cress. Among the flowers are aubrieta, cheiranthus, hesperis and lunaria. The origin of the family name comes from crueus – a cross, all the flowers having four petals, formed in the shape of a cross.

Cucurbitaceae   The gourd family. Almost all of these are grown for their fruiting capacity. Well known members are, cucurbita, cucumis, luffa and lagenaria.

Cupressaceae   The cypress family which takes in cupressus, junipers, libocedrus, thuyas, etc.

Euphorbiaceae   The spurge family consists of many plants of widely differing appearance. Best known as the euphorbias, codiaeum, manihot, acalpha and ricinus.

Gentianaceae There are annual and perennial species in this family, notably gentians and exacum.

Geraniaceae The geranium family takes in the hardy erodium and true geranium as well as the pelargoniums which include those species and varieties used for pot work in greenhouses and for summer bedding.

Gesneriaceae The gesneria family takes in many popular pot plants such as achimenes, episcia, saintpaulia and sinningia.

Gramineae This is the grass family which represents several hundred genera and thousands of species, including such widely differing plants as agrostis, arundinaria, bambusa, coix, festuca, miscanthus, pennisetum and zea, as well as agricultural crops such as barley, oats and wheat.

Iridaceae The iris family provides many attractive ornamental subjects such as crocosmia, crocus, freesia, gladiolus, sparaxis and tritonia.

Labiatae The labiates are of value because of the oils many of them provide. These oils are useful in the preparation of medicines and perfumes included are, mentha, thyme, salvia, hyssop and rosemary.

Leguminosae This again, is an extremely large family varying in size from creeping plants to tall growing subjects such as sweet peas and many shrubs and trees, all of which are capable of producing seed pods, some of which provide food for animals and man. Included are arachis, acacia, pisum (or peas), lupins, cytisus, phaseolus, vicia, lathyrus, laburnum, genista and robinia.

Lilaceae This is another very large family whose members come from very widely separated countries. It takes in various ornamental bulbous subjects with just a few which provide edible crops. They include alliums, camassia, hyacinth, scilla, lilium, tulips, as well as gloriosa, the climbing 'lily'.

Malvaceae	This again is a family of many genera and species, a number of which are known simply as mallows. They include althaea, abutilon, hibiscus, lavatera, malope and sidalcea.
Orchidaceae	A truly large family, containing both terrestial and epiphytic species and varieties, among which are: cypripedium, cymbidium, cattleya, oncidium and vanda.
Palmae	The palm family. This also contains many genera and species among which are, cocos, chamraerops, howea and phoenix.
Papaveraceae	The poppy family. Among other subjects this takes in papavers or poppies, romneya, eschscholtzias and meconopsis.
Primulaceae	The primula family includes both hardy and greenhouse subjects, which take in primroses, polyanthus, cowslips, androsace and cyclamen.
Pteridophyta	This includes ferns, some of the mosses, and selaginella.
Ranunculacaea	The buttercup family contains many ornamental plants such as anemone, clematis, delphinium, helleborus, paeonia, nigella and trollius.
Rosaceae	The rose family consists of between two and three thousand species, many genera, and multitudes of hybrids. While there are no annuals, this group takes in a large number of shrubs and some herbaceous plants such as geums, sanguisorba, potentilla and gillenia, as well as lots of popular shrubs among which are roses, malus, prunus, cotoneaster and pyrus.
Saxifragaceae	The saxifrage family contains many valuable garden plants and shrubs such as bergenia, heuchera, hydrangea, astilbe and ribes.
**Scrophula –
riaceae**	This is the figwort family containing a number of popular plants, shrubs and trees. Among these are antirrhinum, alonsoa, digitalis, linaria, mimulus, veronica, nemesia and calceolaria.
Tropaeolaceae	This is a single genus containing many popular

annual plants, particularly nasturtiums, as well as the perennial Tropaeolum speciosum.

Umbelliferae This is known as the parsley family which is another very large group. Many of the species have commercial uses being added to foods, medicines and drugs as well as having ornamental value. They take in carrots, chervil, celery, parsnip, eryngium and trachymene.

We have mentioned only the most widely known families but some of the lesser known, smaller families are equally important. These include *Begoniaceae, Ericaceae, Polemoniaceae, Acanthaceae, Bignoniaceae, Verbenaceae, Vitaceae*.

Specific Epithets

Once the generic or family name has been confirmed, it is necessary for a specific or Christian name to be applied. The specific epithet of a plant very often gives a good idea of what it looks like. Sometimes, too, these names have more than one descriptive meaning. The following are among the most commonly used epithets:

acaulis	stemless
acris	sharp
affinis	related
alatus	winged
albus or *albo*	white
alternus	alternate
amabilis	lovely
amoenus	pleasing
angulatus	angled
annuus	annual
apiculatus	small-pointed
aquaticus	water plant
arachnoides	cobwebby

arboreus	tree-like
argenteus	silver
aurantiacus	golden
autumnalis	of the autumn
azureaus	sky-blue
baccatus	berried
barbarus	spined or spiked
blandus	tempting, alluring
bullatus	bulbed, inflated
caespitosus	tufted
calcareous	chalky
calceolus	shoe-shaped
callus·	hard skinned
campanulatus	bell-shaped
canaliculatus	channelled
candicans	whitish, hoary
candidus	glittering white
capensis	from South Africa
capitatus	dense head
cardinalis	red
carneus	fleshy, pulpy
caudatus	tailed
cernuus	dropping
cordatus	heart-shaped
decumbens	lying down
denticulatus	small toothed
diffusus	loose, spreading
discolor	two-coloured
dulcis	sweet, pleasing
dumosa	bushy
elegans	choice, elegant
erubescent	blushing
falcatus	sickle-like

fastigiate	steeple-shaped
ferrugineus	rust-coloured
filiformis	thread-like
fimbriatus	fringed, edged
flaccidus	flaccid, languid
flavidus	yellowish
floribundus	with many flowers
foetidus	foul-smelling
fragilis	easily broken
fruticosus	bushy
fulgens	shining
giganteus	huge, giant
glabrus	smooth
glaucus	blue-green
glomeratus	clustered
grandis	great
graveolus	strong-smelling
gymno-	naked
hiemalis	winter-time
hispanica	from Spain
horizontalis	prostrate, growing sideways
hortensis	of the garden
hymeno-	membranous
imbricatus	overlapping
impatiens	enduring
incarnatus	flesh-coloured
indicus	from India
indivisus	undivided
insignis	distinguished
iridifolius	iris-like
italicus	from Italy
japonicus	from Japan
jubatus	crested

junceus	rushy
kalc	beautiful
laciniatus	cut
lactus	milky
laevigatus	smooth
lanceolatus	lance-shaped
lanuginosus	woolly
leuteo	yellow
lilacinus	lilac coloured
linearis	linear formed
lividus	blackish-blue
lobatus	lobe-shaped
luridus	pale yellow
luxurians	exhuberant
macro-	large
maculatus	spotted
magnificus	splendid
major	greater
marginatus	margined
masculus	male
maximus	greatest
medius	intermediate
micro	small, minute
minus	smaller
mollis	tender, pleasant
mucro	sharp, pointed
multi-	many
mutans	varying
nanus	dwarf
niger	black
nutans	nodding
obtusus	blunt
odorus	fragrant

officinalis	official
orbicularis	spherical
ornatus	beautiful
ovatus	egg-shaped
pallidus	pale
palmatus	hand-shaped
palustris	of marshes
parvi-	small
pennatus	winged
perennis	perennial
phaeus	dusky
pictus	ornate
plenus	double
plicatus	folded together
praecox	very early
procumbens	prostrate
pulchellus	very pretty
puniceus	red
pumilis	dwarf
purpureus	purple
quadri-	four
quinatus	divided into five
radicans	rooting
ramosus	branching
reflexus	bent, curved
reginae	queenly
repens	creeping
rigidus	unbending
rotundifolius	round-leaved
rugosus	wrinkled
rupestris	rock-dwelling
sanguineus	blood-red
sativus	cultivated
scandens	climbing

semi-	half
serotinus	late
stellatus	starry
striatus	striped
subulatus	awl-shaped
superbus	splendid
suspensus	hanging
sylvaticus	woodland
tardi-	late
tenuis	slender
turgidus	inflated
tetra	four-square
uniflorus	one-flowered
utilis	useful
vagans	wandering
venustus	lovely
vernalis	spring
versicolor	variously coloured
violaceus	violet
virescens	green
viscosus	sticky
volubilis	changeable
vulgaris	common
wanderus	spreading
xantho-	yellow
yunnanensis	from Yunnan
zebrina	striped
zeylanicus	from Ceylon
zonatus	zonal markings

Common Names

Although it is essential for all plants to have proper or Latin names, so that they can be correctly identified all over the world, a very large number of plants are known by common or nicknames. These are often descriptive of appearance, behaviour, or historical connection. Many are easier to pronounce and remember than the Latin names.

Whilst it would be possible to compile an almost limitless list, the following are the common names of some of our most popular flowers with their Latin equivalents, although in some cases the common or English name applies to only one of the species in the family:

Adam's Needle	*yucca*
Amaryllis	*hippeastrum*
Baby's Breath	*gypsophila*
Bachelor's Buttons	*ranunculus*
Beard Tongue	*penstemon*
Bell Flower	*campanula*
Bergamot	*monarda*
Bistort	*polygonum*
Bouncing Bet	*saponaria*
Brompton Stock	*matthiola*
Bugle Lily	*watsonia*
Bleeding Heart	*dicentra*

Camomile	*anthemis*
Canary Creeper	*tropaeolum*
Capers	*capparis*
Carnation	*dianthus*
Catnip	*nepeta*
Century Plant	*agave*
Christmas Rose	*helleborus*
Chinese Lantern	*physalis*
Cheddar Pink	*dianthus*
Chinaman's Breeches	*dicentra*
Columbine	*aquilegia*
Cone Flower	*rudbeckia*
Cowslip	*primula*
Cupid's Dart	*catananche*
Cypress Vine	*quamoclit*
Daffodil	*narcissus*
Daisy	*bellis*
Dame's Violet	*hesperis*
Dutchman's Breeches	*dicentra*
Evening Primrose	*oenothera*
Fleabane	*erigeron*
False Hellebore	*veratrum*
Forget-Me-Not	*myosotis*
Foxglove	*digitalis*
Fleur-de-Lys	*iris*
Feverfew	*pyrethrum*
Gloxinia	*sinningia*
Gold Dust	*alysum*
Geranium	*pelargonium*
Guernsey Lily	*nerine*
Granny's Bonnet	*aquilegia*
Harebell	*campanula*
Heartsease	*viola*
Hollyhock	*althaea*

Jacobean Lily	*sprekelia*
Jacob's Ladder	*polemonium*
King Cup	*caltha*
King's Spur	*delphinium*
Lady-in-Bath	*dicentra*
Leopard's Bane	*doronicum*
Lily of the Valley	*convallaria*
Loosestrife	*lysimachia*
Lyre Flower	*dicentra*
Marigold	*tagetes*
Michaelmas Daisy	*aster*
Mignonette	*reseda*
Mistletoe	*viscum*
Meadow Rue	*chalictrum*
Mullein	*verbascum*
Old Man	*artemesia*
Oxlip	*primula*
Pasque Flower	*pulsatilla*
Pink	*dianthus*
Plume Poppy	*macleaya*
Poinsettia	*euphorbia*
Polyanthus	*primula*
Poppy	*papaver*
Pot Marigold	*calendula*
Primrose	*primula*
Quamash	*camassia*
Red Hot Poker	*kniphofia*
Rocket	*hesperis*
Rose	*rosa*
Saffron	*crocus*

Sage	*salvia*
Siberian Wallflower	*cheiranthus*
Silk Grass	*yucca*
Snakeshead	*fritillaria*
Snapdragon	*antirrhinum*
Snowdrop	*galanthus*
Spurge	*euphorbia*
St James's Lily	*sprekelia*
Stock	*matthiola*
Sunflower	*helianthus*
Sweet Pea	*lathyrus*
Sweet William	*dianthus*
Sword Lily	*gladiolus*
Tickseed	*coreopsis*
Valerian	*kentranthus*
Vervain	*verbena*
Violet	*viola*
Wake Robin	*trillium*
Wallflower	*cheiranthus*
Windflower	*anemone*
Woad	*isatis*
Yarrow	*achillea*
Zebra Grass	*miscanthus*

Glossary of Botanical Terms

adventitious roots or shoots	Those arising in other than normal places.
annual	A plant which germinates, flowers, seeds and dies within one season.
anther	The pollen-bearing part of the stamen.
aril	An outer covering of the seed.
aromatic	Fragrant, as applying to parts other than the flowers
awl-shaped	Sharp and narrow.
axil	The upper angle between the main stem and a leaf stem.
baccata	Fleshy or berry-like.
beak	A prominent point on a seed.
biennial	A plant which germinates, flowers, seeds and dies within two seasons.
bigeneric hybrid	A plant obtained by crossing two genera.
bisexual	Flower possessing both stamens and pistil.
blade	The main expanded part of a leaf.
bract	A modified leaf, often associated with the flower.
bulbils	Small bulbs arising from around the main bulb.
bullate	Having a pimpled or blistered surface.
bush	A shrub; a tree without a basal trunk.
calcifuge	Intolerant of lime.
callus	Tissue from a cut or wound from which roots will issue.
calyx	A pod or fruit formed by several capsules.

clasping	A leaf wholly or partly clasping the stem.
composite	Compound; comprised of a number of similar but distinct parts.
cordate	Heart-shaped as seen in some leaves.
corm	A solid bulb-like structure without scales.
corolla	The parts of a flower immediately within the calyx.
corymb	A flat-topped cluster of flowers.
cotyledon	The seed leaf, primary leaf or pair of leaves.
cruciform	Cross-shaped; four petals making a cross.
cultivar	Hybrids or variations arising under cultivation.
deciduous	Falling of leaves as in non-evergreen plants.
dehiscence	The opening of the seed pod.
diffuse	Open growth or of loose habit.
dioecious	Unisexual; having staminate and pistillate flowers on separate plants.
diploid	A plant with two sets of chromosomes.
ecology	The study of plants in relation to their environment.
fasciated	Abnormality of stem or flower which appears flattened.
filament	A thread; the stalk of an anther.
florets	Small flowers making up a truss.
furrowed	Marked with grooves lengthwise.
glaucous	Dull grey-green or blue-green.
glomerate	Dense, as seen in clusters.
habitat	The natural home of a plant.
herb	A non-woody perennial that dies down to the ground in winter but remains alive below ground.
host plant	A plant on which another plant grows parasitically.
hybrid	A plant resulting from the pollination of one cultivar by another.
internode	The stem between two consecutive nodes.
involucre	A whorl of bracts around the stem below a flower

	cluster.
irregular	Describing flowers with parts of different size or shape.
keel	The two lower petals in leguminous plants.
laciniate	Leaves deeply cut into narrow lobes.
lateral	A side branch or shoot.
legume	The seed pod of a leguminous plant.
linear	Long and evenly narrow leaves.
lobe	Part of a leaf or petal which is divided partially or almost wholly.
marginate	Edged in a different colour or texture.
monoecious	Having staminate and pistillate flowers on the same plant.
monotypic	A plant of which there is only one species in the genus.
mycorrhiza	The association of a plant's roots with a fungus.
node	A joint where a bud or leaf is produced.
ovary	The part of the pistil bearing the ovule.
palmate	Leaves lobed in the shape of a hand.
panicle	Flower clusters or branching racemes.
plumule	The embryo terminal bud in a seed.
pubescent	Having a covering of down.
radiate	Spreading from a centre, as with ray florets.
radical	The first root in a seedling.
ray	The outer or marginal florets of daisy-like flowers.
rhizome	The underground root-stock of some plants.
runner	A slender trailing shoot which often roots at the nodes.
sagittate	Leaves with arrow-like heads.
scape	Leafless stem rising from the ground and terminating in a flower.
sepal	One of the separate parts of the calyx.
segment	A single leaf or petal.
sessile	Without a stalk; sitting on a leaf.

species	A plant which comes true from seed.
spike	An elongated, indefinite flower cluster.
stamen	The male pollen-bearing part of the flower.
staminate	With stamens but no pistil.
stigma	The part of the pistil that receives pollen.
stipule	Basal appendages of a leaf stalk.
stolon	A stem issuing from a plant horizontally below ground.
succulent	A plant with soft fleshy leaves and stems.
tapering	Leaves and petals that gradually diminish in width.
tendril	A stem or petiole by which a plant twists and clings.
tomentose	Thickly pubescent or woolly.
umbel	A flower head on which the pedicels are of equal length.
variety	Differing from the species but insufficiently so to warrant the status of a separate species.
whorl	A plant with at least three leaves or flower stems at one node around the stem.
woolly	Covered with many soft long hairs.
zonal	Flowers or leaves with a band of a different colour.

Patron Saints

Countries, cities, the arts and crafts all have their patron saints and there are several saints who are associated with gardens and plants. St Dorothy was martyred in Cappadocia about the year AD 300 for being a Christian. It is said that at her trial a lawyer mockingly asked her to send him fruit and flowers from the garden of Heaven. On the day of her execution he received roses and apples from a messenger, even though it was in the depths of winter. Also St Phoecas, St Veronica, St Chrysanthus, St Bernard's Lily, St James Lily and St Brigid Anemone must be taken into account.

The patron saint of gardeners is thought by many to be St Fiacre, who lived about the years AD 600 to 690. He was an Irish missionary who travelled to Europe about that time. He settled in France on the banks of the River Marne in Normany, where he led the religious life of a hermit in forest solitude. Inhabitants of the district began to seek him out to learn the Christian faith, but their hunger and hardships so troubled him that he cleared the land and cultivated the soil in order to grow corn and vegetables for their needs. His crops were so abundant that his fame spread and he became honoured for his work, the spade being his own special symbol.

The cult of St Fiacre grew steadily in France, reaching its peak during the seventeenth century, almost 1,000 years after his death. His shrine at La Brie became famous, and he was the favoured saint of both rich and poor. There does not appear to be a tree, shrub or flower which carries his name, although there was once an alpine strawberry named St Fiacre.

For Further Reading

Encyclopaedia of Gardening, J.C. Loudon, 1822.
A History of English Gardens, G.W. Johnson, 1829.
History of Gardening in England, Hon. A. Amherst, 1896.
English Gardens, H.A. Tipping, 1925.
Old Fashioned Flowers, Sacheverell Sitwell, 1948.
The Coming of the Flowers, H.M. Anderson, 1950.
Flowers and their History, Alice Coates, 1968.
Flowers and Trees in Tudor England, C. Robinson, 1972.